2

Second Grade
Essentials

Thinking Kids®
Carson-Dellosa Publishing LLC
Greensboro, North Carolina

Thinking Kids®
An imprint of Carson-Dellosa Publishing LLC
P.O. Box 35665
Greensboro, NC 27425 USA

ISBN 978-1-4838-3819-9

01-135171151

Table of Contents

INTRODUCTION

Welcome to the *Essentials* series!

Building a strong foundation is an essential part of your child's everyday success. This series features a variety of activity pages that make learning fun, keeping your child engaged and entertained at the same time. These colorful workbooks will help children meet important proficiency standards with activities that strengthen their basic skills, math, and reading.

With the *Essentials* series, learning isn't just contained to the pages of the workbook. Each activity offers "One Step Further," a suggestion for children to continue the learning activity on their own. This encourages children to take what they've learned and apply it to everyday situations, reinforcing their comprehension of the activity while exploring the world around them, preparing them with the skills needed to succeed in the 21st century.

These books provide an outstanding educational experience and important learning tools to prepare your child for the future. The *Essentials* series offers hours of educational entertainment that will make your child want to come back for more!

Basic Skills

All About Me!

Directions: Fill in the blanks to tell all about you!

Name _____
          (First)   (Last)

Address _____

City _____ State _____

Phone number _____

Age _____

Places I have visited: _____

_____

_____

_____

My favorite vacation: _____

_____

_____

One Step Further
What else could you write about yourself?
Include your favorite activities.

Parts of a Book

A book has many parts. The **title** is the name of the book. The **author** is the person who wrote the words. The **illustrator** is the person who drew the pictures. The **table of contents** is located at the beginning to list what is in the book. The **glossary** is a little dictionary in the back to help you with unfamiliar words. Books are often divided into smaller sections of information called **chapters**.

Directions: Look at one of your books. Write the parts you see below.

The title of my book is _____ .

The author is _____ .

The illustrator is _____ .

My book has a table of contents.   Yes or No

My book has a glossary.   Yes or No

My book is divided into chapters.   Yes or No

One Step Further
What else can you tell about your book?
What category would it fit into at the library?

BASIC SKILLS

ABC Order

Directions: Put the words in ABC order on the bags.

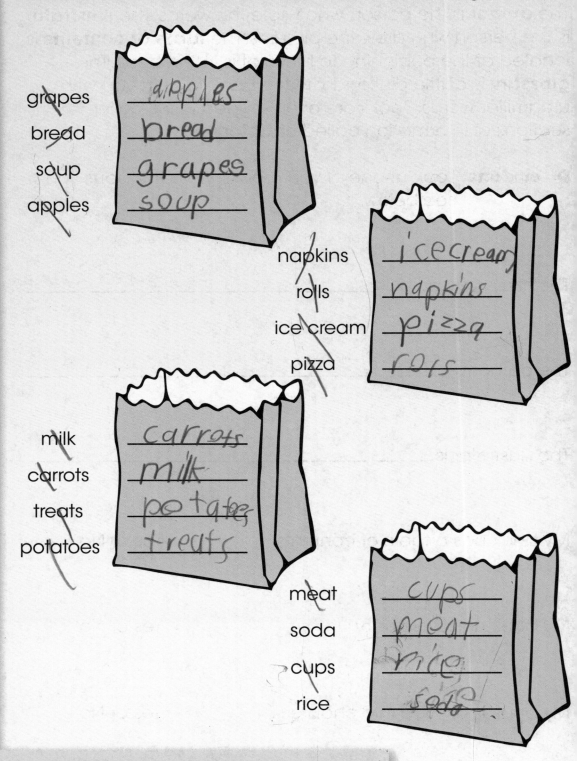

grapes
bread
soup
apples

apples
bread
grapes
soup

napkins
rolls
ice cream
pizza

ice cream
napkins
pizza
rolls

milk
carrots
treats
potatoes

carrots
milk
potatoes
treats

meat
soda
cups
rice

cups
meat
rice
soda

One Step Further

At the grocery store, look in your cart.
Put the items in ABC order.

BASIC SKILLS

ABC Order

Directions: Write these words in order. If two words start with the same letter, look at the second letter in each word.

Example: lamb   **Lamb** is first because **a** comes before **i**   **light**   in the alphabet.

tree   _branch_

branch   _leaf_

leaf   _tree_

dish   _bone_

dog   _dish_

bone   _dog_

rain   _cloud_

umbrella   _umbrella_

cloud   _rain_

One Step Further

Choose three objects from your bookbag.
Put them in ABC order.

BASIC SKILLS

ABC Order

If the first letters of two words are the same, look at the second letters in both words. If the second letters are the same, look at the third letters.

Directions: Write 1, 2, 3, or 4 on the lines in each row to put the words in ABC order. The first one has been done for you.

1. __1__ candy   __2__ carrot   __4__ duck   __3__ dance

2. __2__ cold   __4__ hot   __1__ carry   __3__ hit

3. __2__ flash   __1__ fan   __3__ fun   __4__ garden

4. __2__ seat   __4__ sun   __1__ saw   __3__ sit

5. __3__ row   __1__ ring   __2__ rock   __4__ run

6. __2__ truck   __3__ turn   __4__ twin   __1__ talk

One Step Further

Write four words. Ask a friend to put them in ABC order.

ABC Order

Kwan likes to make rhymes. Help Kwan think of rhyming words.

Rhyming is my game.

Directions: Write three words in ABC order that rhyme with each word Kwan wrote.

cap   bet   bill

_____   _____   _____

_____   _____   _____

_____   _____   _____

dog   man   hat

_____   _____   _____

_____   _____   _____

_____   _____   _____

Directions: Write a short poem using some of the rhyming words you wrote.

_____

_____

_____

_____

One Step Further

Choose two rhyming words from this page. Can you find both objects in your home?

BASIC SKILLS

Syllables

Words are made up of parts called **syllables**. Each syllable has a vowel sound. One way to count syllables is to clap as you say the word.

Example:
cat	one clap	one syllable
table	two claps	two syllables
butterfly	three claps	three syllables

Directions: "Clap out" the words below. Write how many syllables each word has.

movie _____   dog _____

piano _____   basket _____

tree _____   swimmer _____

bicycle _____   rainbow _____

sun _____   paper _____

cabinet _____   picture _____

One Step Further

Clap as you say your first name out loud.
How many syllables does your name have?

BASIC SKILLS

Syllables

Dividing a word into syllables can help you read a new word. You also might divide syllables when you are writing if you run out of space on a line.

Many words contain two consonants that are next to each other. A word can usually be divided between the consonants.

Directions: Divide each word into two syllables. The first one has been done for you.

kitten   _____ **kit   ten** _____

lumber   _____

batter   _____

winter   _____

funny   _____

harder   _____

dirty   _____

sister   _____

little   _____

BASIC SKILLS

One Step Further
What is the name of your school?
How many syllables does it have?

Syllables

One way to help you read a word you don't know is to divide it into parts called **syllables**. Every syllable has a vowel sound.

Directions: Say the words. Write the number of syllables.

straw • ber • ry

bird _____   rabbit _____

apple _____   elephant _____

balloon _____   family _____

basketball _____   fence _____

breakfast _____   ladder _____

block _____   open _____

candy _____   puddle _____

popcorn _____   Saturday _____

One Step Further

Find a book. Choose a sentence and divide each word into syllables.

BASIC SKILLS

Syllables

When a double consonant is used in the middle of a word, the word can usually be divided between the consonants.

Directions: Look at the words in the word box. Divide each word into two syllables. Leave space between each syllable. One is done for you.

butter	pillow	chatter	kitten	mitten	happy
dinner	puppy	letter	ladder	yellow	summer

but   ter

_____   _____   _____

_____   _____   _____

_____   _____   _____

_____   _____   _____

Many words are divided between two consonants that are not alike.

Directions: Look at the words in the word box. Divide each word into two syllables. One is done for you.

window	barber	winter	number	picture	candle
mister	doctor	sister	pencil	carpet	under

win   dow

_____   _____   _____

_____   _____   _____

_____   _____   _____

BASIC SKILLS

One Step Further
Walk around your neighborhood.
Divide all the objects you see into syllables.

Second Grade Essentials

Syllables

Directions: Write 1 or 2 on the line to tell how many syllables are in each word. If the word has two syllables, draw a line between the syllables.

Example: sup|per

dog	_____	timber	_____
bedroom	_____	cat	_____
slipper	_____	street	_____
tree	_____	chalk	_____
batter	_____	blanket	_____
chair	_____	marker	_____
fish	_____	brush	_____

One Step Further

Can you name a word that has three syllables? Four syllables?

Learning Dictionary Skills

A **dictionary** is a book that gives the meaning of words. It also tells how words sound. Words in a dictionary are in ABC order. That makes them easier to find. A picture dictionary lists a word, a picture of the word, and its meaning.

Directions: Look at this page from a picture dictionary. Then, answer the questions.

baby

A very
young child.

band

A group of people
who play music.

bank

A place where
money is kept.

---

bark

The sound a
dog makes.

berry

A small,
juicy fruit.

board

A flat piece
of wood.

1. What is a small, juicy fruit?_____

2. What is a group of people who play music?_____

3. What is the name for a very young child?_____

4. What is a flat piece of wood called?_____

One Step Further

Look up all these words in a dictionary.
What is the definition your dictionary gives?

Learning Dictionary Skills

Directions: Look at this page from a picture dictionary. Then, answer the questions.

safe

A metal box.

sea

A body of water.

seed

The beginning of a plant.

---

sheep

An animal that has wool.

store

A place where items are sold.

skate

A shoe with wheels or a blade on it.

1. What kind of animal has wool?_____

2. What do you call a shoe with wheels on it?_____

3. What is a place where items are sold?_____

4. When a plant starts, what is it called?_____

One Step Further
Think of a word and look it up in the dictionary. Read the definition.

BASIC SKILLS

Learning Dictionary Skills

Directions: Look at this page from a picture dictionary. Then, answer the questions.

table

Furniture with legs and a flat top.

tail

A slender part that is on the back of an animal.

teacher

A person who teaches lessons.

---

telephone

A machine that sends and receives sounds.

ticket

A paper slip or card.

tiger

An animal with stripes.

1. Who is a person who teaches lessons?_____

2. What is the name of an animal with stripes?_____

3. What is a piece of furniture with legs and a flat top?

_____

4. What is the definition of a ticket?_____

_____

One Step Further

Choose a word that starts with the letter **t**.
Write the definition in your own words.

BASIC SKILLS

Stuffed Animals

Kate and Oralia like to collect and trade stuffed animals.

Directions: Draw two stuffed animals that are alike and two that are different.

Alike

Different

BASIC SKILLS

One Step Further

Do you have two stuffed animals that are alike? Can you find two that are different?

Shell Homes

Directions: Read about shells. Then, answer the questions.

Shells are the homes of some animals. Snails live in shells on the land. Clams live in shells in the water. Clam shells open. Snail shells stay closed. Both shells keep the animals safe.

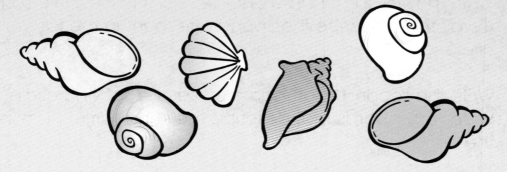

1. (Circle the correct answer.) Snails live in shells on the

   water.   land.

2. (Circle the correct answer.) Clam shells are different from snail shells because

   they open.

   they stay closed.

3. Write one way both shells are the same. _____

   _____

   _____

One Step Further
Draw a picture of a pretty seashell.
Do you have a collection of seashells?

Venn Diagram

A **Venn diagram** is a diagram that shows how two things are the same and different.

Directions: Choose two outdoor sports. Then, follow the instructions to complete the Venn diagram.

1. Write the first sport name under the first circle. Write some words that describe the sport. Write them in the first circle.

2. Write the second sport name under the second circle. Write some words that describe the sport. Write them in the circle.

3. Where the two circles overlap, write some words that describe both sports.

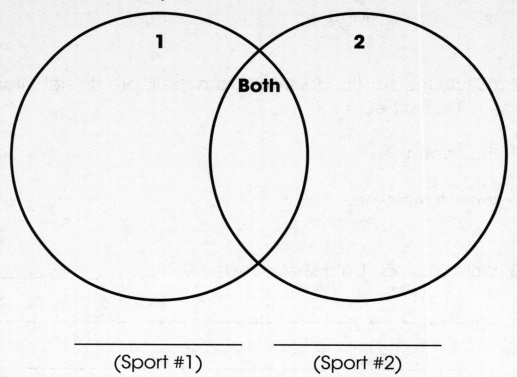

1   Both   2

_____   _____
(Sport #1)   (Sport #2)

One Step Further
Create another Venn diagram comparing two subjects in school.

Dina and Dina

Directions: Read the story. Then, complete the Venn diagram, telling how Dina, the duck, is the same or different than Dina, the girl.

One day in the library, Dina found a story about a duck named Dina!

My name is Dina. I am a duck, and I like to swim. When I am not swimming, I walk on land or fly. I have two feet and two eyes. My feathers keep me warm. Ducks can be different colors. I am gray, brown, and black. I really like being a duck. It is fun.

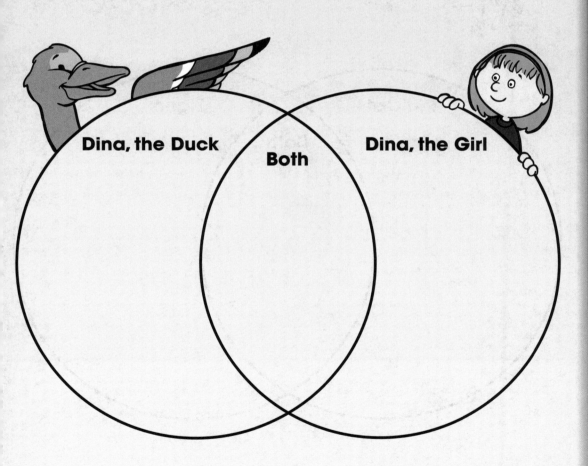

Dina, the Duck   **Both**   **Dina, the Girl**

One Step Further

Choose an animal. How are you different from the animal? How are you the same?

Cats and Tigers

Directions: Read about cats and tigers. Then, complete the Venn diagram, telling how they are the same and different.

Tigers are a kind of cat. Pet cats and tigers both have fur. Pet cats are small and tame. Tigers are large and wild.

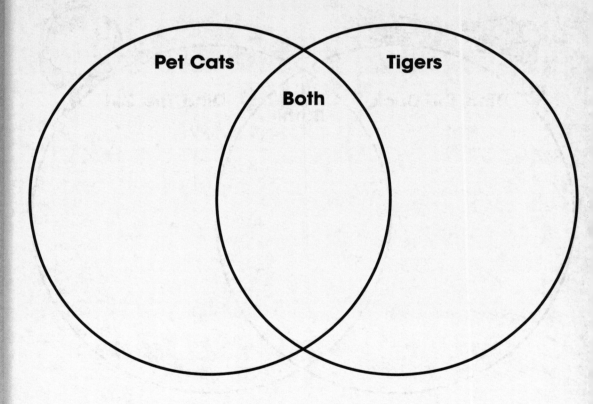

Pet Cats   Tigers

Both

One Step Further
Name at least two more differences between pet cats and tigers.

Bluebirds and Parrots

Directions: Read about parrots and bluebirds. Then, complete the Venn diagram, telling how they are the same and different.

Bluebirds and parrots are both birds. Bluebirds and parrots can fly. They both have beaks. Parrots can live inside a cage. Bluebirds must live outdoors.

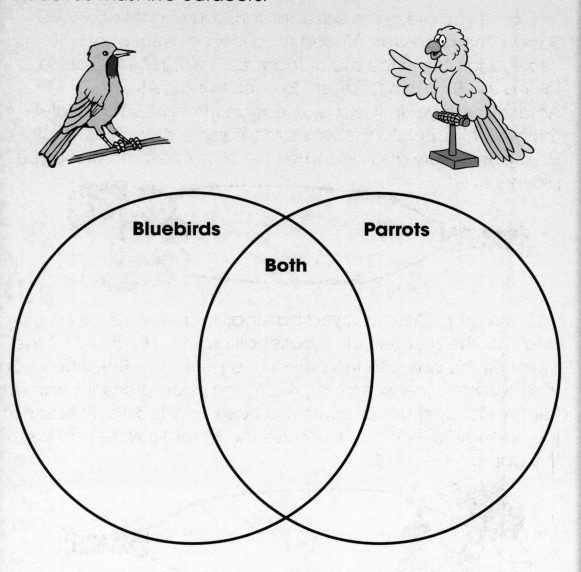

Bluebirds

Both

Parrots

One Step Further

Describe the birds you see outside. How are they different from bluebirds and parrots?

BASIC SKILLS

Heavy Hitters

Fiction is a make-believe story. **Nonfiction** is a true story.

Directions: Read the stories about two famous baseball players. Then, write **fiction** or **nonfiction** in the baseball bats.

Even if you are not a baseball fan, you might know who Jackie Robinson was. African American players were not allowed to play in the major leagues. Then, in 1947, Jackie joined the Brooklyn Dodgers. He was the first African American player in the major leagues. People said hateful things to him. But Jackie was strong and did not fight back. He made history and became one of the best major league players ever!

The Mighty Casey played baseball for the Mudville Nine and was the greatest of all baseball players. He could hit the cover off the ball with the power of a hurricane. But, when the Mudville Nine was losing 4–2 in the championship game, Mighty Casey struck out with the bases loaded. There was no joy in Mudville that day, because the Mudville Nine had lost the game.

One Step Further

Do you know any other famous baseball players? Tell a story about baseball.

Tornado Tips

Directions: Read about tornadoes. Then, follow the instructions.

A tornado begins over land with strong winds and thunderstorms. The spinning air becomes a funnel. It can cause damage. If you are inside, go to the lowest floor of the building. A basement is a safe place. A bathroom or closet in the middle of a building can be a safe place, too. If you are outside, lie in a ditch. Remember, tornadoes are dangerous.

Write five facts about tornadoes.

1. _____
_____

2. _____
_____

3. _____
_____

4. _____
_____

5. _____
_____

BASIC SKILLS

One Step Further
What do you do when it's storming outside?
When was the last time it stormed?

Hercules

The **setting** is where a story takes place. The **characters** are the people in a story or play.

Directions: Read about Hercules. Then, answer the questions.

Hercules was born in the warm Atlantic Ocean. He was a very small and weak baby. He wanted to be the strongest hurricane in the world. But he had one problem. He couldn't blow 75-mile-per-hour winds. Hercules blew and blew in the ocean, until one day, his sister, Hola, told him it would be more fun to be a breeze than a hurricane. Hercules agreed. It was a breeze to be a breeze!

1. What is the setting of the story? _____

2. Who are the characters? _____

3. What is the problem? _____

_____

4. How does Hercules solve his problem? _____

_____

One Step Further
Write a story about a stormy day.
Is your story fiction or nonfiction?

The Fourth of July

Directions: Read each story. Then, write whether it is fiction or nonfiction.

One sunny day in July, a dog named Stan ran away from home. He went up one street and down the other looking for fun, but all the yards were empty. Where was everybody? Stan kept walking until he heard the sound of band music and happy people. Stan walked faster until he got to Central Street. There he saw men, women, children, and dogs getting ready to walk in a parade. It was the Fourth of July!

Fiction or nonfiction? _____

Americans celebrate the Fourth of July every year, because it is the birthday of the United States of America. On July 4, 1776, the United States got its independence from Great Britain. Today, Americans celebrate this holiday with parades, picnics, and fireworks as they proudly wave the red, white, and blue American flag.

Fiction or nonfiction? _____

One Step Further
What do you do to celebrate the Fourth of July?

Which Is It?

Directions: Read about fiction and nonfiction books. Then, follow the instructions.

There are many kinds of books. Some books have make-believe stories about princesses and dragons. Some books contain poetry and rhymes, like Mother Goose. These are fiction.

Some books contain facts about space and plants. And still other books have stories about famous people in history, like Abraham Lincoln. These are nonfiction.

Write **F** for fiction and **NF** for nonfiction.

_____ 1. nursery rhyme

_____ 2. fairy tale

_____ 3. true-life story of a famous athlete

_____ 4. Aesop's fables

_____ 5. dictionary entry about foxes

_____ 6. weather report

_____ 7. story about a talking tree

_____ 8. story about how a tadpole becomes a frog

One Step Further
What books do you most like to read, fiction or nonfiction? Why?

Games!

A **fact** is something that can be proven. An **opinion** is a feeling or belief about something and cannot be proven.

Directions: Read these sentences about different games. Then, write **F** next to each fact and **O** next to each opinion.

_____ 1. Tennis is cool!

_____ 2. There are red and black markers in a Checkers game.

_____ 3. In football, a touchdown is worth six points.

_____ 4. Being a goalie in soccer is easy.

_____ 5. A yo-yo moves on a string.

_____ 6. June's sister looks like the queen on the card.

_____ 7. The six kids need three more players for a baseball team.

_____ 8. Table tennis is more fun than court tennis.

One Step Further
What is your favorite sport? Name a fact and an opinion about that sport.

Recycling

Directions: Read about recycling. Then, follow the instructions.

What do you throw away every day? What could you do with these things? You could change an old greeting card into a new card. You could make a puppet with an old paper bag. Old buttons make great refrigerator magnets. You can plant seeds in plastic cups. Cardboard tubes make perfect rockets. So, use your imagination!

Write **F** next to each fact and **O** next to each opinion.

_____ Cardboard tubes are ugly.

_____ Buttons can be made into refrigerator magnets.

_____ An old greeting card can be changed into a new card.

_____ Paper-bag puppets are cute.

_____ Seeds can be planted in plastic cups.

_____ Rockets can be made from cardboard tubes.

One Step Further
What else could you recycle?
Try different craft projects with a friend.

An Owl Story

Directions: Read the story. Then, follow the instructions.

My name is Owen Owl, and I am a bird. I go to Nocturnal School. Our teacher is Mr. Screech Owl. In his class, I learned that owls are birds and can sleep all day and hunt at night. Some of us live in nests in trees. In North America, it is against the law to harm owls. I like being an owl!

Write **F** next to each fact and **O** next to each opinion.

_____ 1. No one can harm owls in North America.

_____ 2. It would be great if owls could talk.

_____ 3. Owls sleep all day.

_____ 4. Some owls sleep in nests.

_____ 5. Mr. Screech Owl is a good teacher.

_____ 6. Owls are birds.

_____ 7. Owen Owl would be a good friend.

_____ 8. Owls hunt at night.

One Step Further
Read a book about owls.
Tell a friend about everything you learned.

BASIC SKILLS

Henrietta the Humpback

Directions: Read the story. Then, follow the instructions.

My name is Henrietta, and I am a humpback whale. I live in cold seas in the summer and warm seas in the winter. My long flippers are used to move forward and backward. I like to eat fish. Sometimes, I show off by leaping out of the water. Would you like to be a humpback whale?

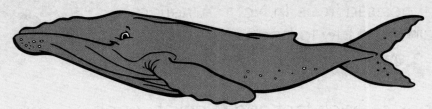

Write **F** next to each fact and **O** next to each opinion.

_____ 1. Being a humpback whale is fun.

_____ 2. Humpback whales live in cold seas during the summer.

_____ 3. Whales are fun to watch.

_____ 4. Humpback whales use their flippers to move forward and backward.

_____ 5. Henrietta is a great name for a whale.

_____ 6. Leaping out of water would be hard.

_____ 7. Humpback whales like to eat fish.

_____ 8. Humpback whales show off by leaping out of the water.

One Step Further
Name other animals that might live near a humpback whale.

Outdoor/Indoor Games

Classifying is putting things that are alike into groups.

Directions: Draw an **X** on the games you can play indoors. Circle the objects used for outdoor games.

One Step Further
Outdoor games are active. Indoor games are quiet. Which do you like best?

Classifying

Directions: Write each word from the word box on the correct line.

baby	goose	family	policeman
uncle	whale	kangaroo	
donkey	grandfather	fox	

people   **animals**

_____ _____

_____ _____

_____ _____

_____ _____

_____ _____

One Step Further

What other words could go in the people category? In the animal category?

Animals

Directions: Use a **red** crayon to circle the names of three animals that would make good pets. Use a **blue** crayon to circle the names of three wild animals. Use an orange crayon to circle the two animals that live on a farm.

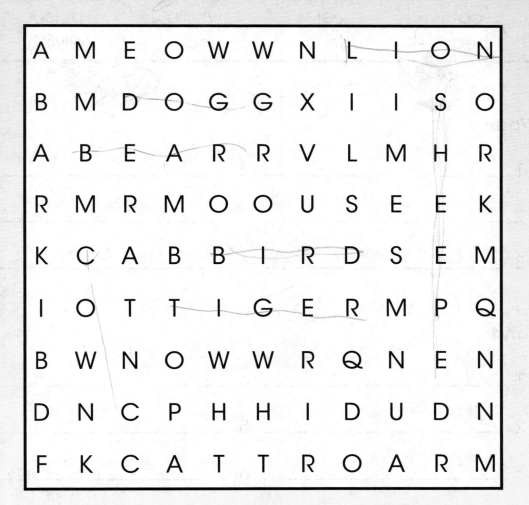

| BEAR | CAT | LION | SHEEP | BIRD | DOG | COW | TIGER |

```
A  M  E  O  W  W  N  L  I  O  N
B  M  D  O  G  G  X  I  I  S  O
A  B  E  A  R  R  V  L  M  H  R
R  M  R  M  O  O  U  S  E  E  K
K  C  A  B  B  I  R  D  S  E  M
I  O  T  T  I  G  E  R  M  P  Q
B  W  N  O  W  W  R  Q  N  E  N
D  N  C  P  H  H  I  D  U  D  N
F  K  C  A  T  T  R  O  A  R  M
```

BASIC SKILLS

One Step Further
Create a word search of your own.
Include items you use to get ready for bed.

Second Grade Essentials

Animal Habitats

Directions: Read the article. Then, write each animal's name under **Water** or **Land** to tell where it lives.

Animals live in different habitats. A habitat is the place of an animal's natural home. Many animals live on land and others live in water. Most animals that live in water breathe with gills. Animals that live on land breathe with lungs.

fish	shrimp	giraffe	dog
cat	eel	whale	horse
bear	deer	shark	jellyfish

Water

1. _____   4. _____

2. _____   5. _____

3. _____   6. _____

Land

1. _____   4. _____

2. _____   5. _____

3. _____   6. _____

One Step Further

Name more animals that live on land. Which of those animals do you see most often?

Cows Give Us Milk

Directions: Read the article. Answer the questions.

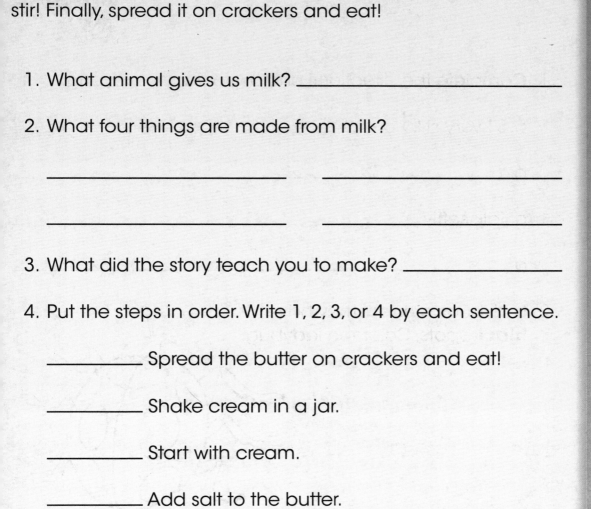

Cows live on farms. The farmer milks the cow to get milk. Many things are made from milk. We make ice cream, sour cream, cottage cheese, and butter from milk. Butter is fun to make! You can learn to make your own butter. First, you need cream. Put the cream in a jar and shake it. Then, you need to pour off the liquid. Next, you put the butter in a bowl. Add a little salt and stir! Finally, spread it on crackers and eat!

1. What animal gives us milk? _____

2. What four things are made from milk?

   _____   _____

   _____   _____

3. What did the story teach you to make? _____

4. Put the steps in order. Write 1, 2, 3, or 4 by each sentence.

   _____ Spread the butter on crackers and eat!

   _____ Shake cream in a jar.

   _____ Start with cream.

   _____ Add salt to the butter.

BASIC SKILLS

One Step Further

Try the recipe for making butter. How did it turn out? What do you use butter for?

How to Treat a Ladybug

Directions: Read about how to treat ladybugs. Then, follow the instructions.

Ladybugs are shy. If you see a ladybug, sit very still. Hold out your arm. Maybe the ladybug will fly to you. If it does, talk softly. Do not touch it. It will fly away when it is ready.

1. Complete the directions on how to treat a ladybug.

   a. Sit very still.

   b. _____

   c. Talk softly.

   d. _____

2. Ladybugs are **red**. They have **black** spots. Color the ladybug.

One Step Further

Go outside and look for a ladybug.
See if you can get it to land on your arm.

Find the Books

Directions: Use the clues to help the children find their books. Draw a line from each child's name to the correct book.

Brett   **Aki**   **Lorenzo**   **Kate**   **Zac**   **Oralia**

Children	Books
Brett	jokes
Aki	cakes
Lorenzo	monsters
Kate	games
Zac	flags
Oralia	space

Clues

1. Lorenzo likes jokes.
2. Kate likes to bake.
3. Oralia likes faraway places.
4. Aki does not like monsters or flags.
5. Zac does not like space or monsters.
6. Brett does not like games, jokes, or cakes.

One Step Further

What type of book do you like most?
Name three books you've recently read.

BASIC SKILLS

Sports

Children all over the world like to play sports. They like many different kinds of sports: football, soccer, basketball, softball, in-line skating, swimming, and more.

Directions: Read the clues. Draw dots on the chart to match the children with their sports.

	swimming	football	soccer	basketball	baseball	in-line skating
J.J.		●				
Zoe						●
Andy				●		
Amber			●			
Raul					●	
Sierra	●					

Clues

1. Zoe hates football, but loves in-line skating.
2. Andy likes basketball.
3. Raul likes to pitch in his favorite sport.
4. J.J. likes to play what Zoe hates.
5. Amber is good at kicking the ball to her teammates.
6. Sierra needs a pool for her favorite sport.

One Step Further

Which is your favorite sport from this list?
Which is your least favorite?

Reading

Batter Up!

What did Bobby yell to the batter?

Directions: To find out, say the name of each picture. On the line, write the letter that you hear at the beginning of each picture.

H I Y A

H O M E R R N !

One Step Further

Go outside and play baseball with a friend.
See how far you can hit the ball.

Tic-Tac-Toe

Directions: Find the three pictures in each game whose names begin with the same sound. Draw a line through them.

One Step Further

Play a game of tic-tac-toe with a friend.
The winner gets to choose the next game.

Consonant Blends

Consonant blends are two or three consonant letters in a word whose sounds combine, or blend.

Example: br, fr, gr, pr, tr

Directions: Look at each picture. Say its name. Write the blend you hear at the beginning of each word.

_____   _____   _____

_____   _____   _____

   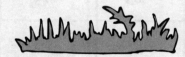   

_____   _____   _____

One Step Further

Crayon contains a consonant blend. Can you name another word with a blend?

Blend Match-Up

Directions: Say the name of each picture. Draw lines to match the pictures that have the same beginning blend.

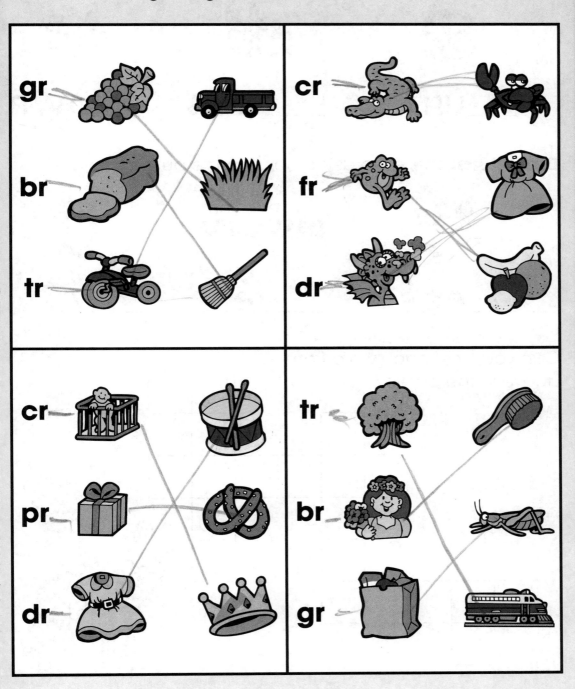

READING

One Step Further
Choose three pictures from this page. Make up a story about them.

Crown the King

Directions: Write the beginning blend on the line. These words go across in the puzzle.

1.

3.

5.

___um   ___apes   ___own

Directions: These words go down in the puzzle.

1.

2.

4.

___ess   ___een   ___y

Can you write each word from above in the puzzle?

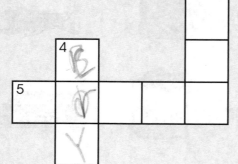

One Step Further

Have a contest with a friend. Who can write the most words that have a blend?

Nothing but Net

Directions: Write the missing consonant blends.

mp	dr	lp	nk	st	sk	nd	gr	sn	nt	fr	sl

1. "My ___ ___ eakers he ___ ___ me run very fa ___ ___!" exclaimed Jim Shooz.

2. "I really like to ___ ___ ibble the ball," announced Dub L. Dribble.

3. Team captain ___ ___ y-High Hook can easily ___ ___ am

    du ___ ___ the basketball into the net.

4. Will Kenny Dooit make an extra poi ___ ___ with his

    ___ ___ ee throw?

5. Harry Leggs can ju ___ ___ at lea ___ ___ four feet off

    the ___ ___ ound.

6. Wow! Willie Makeit finally caught the ball on the

    rebou ___ ___!

7. "I cannot tell which team will win at the e ___ ___ of the game," decided Ed G. Nerves.

8. "You silly boy! Of course, the team with the mo ___ ___

    poi ___ ___ s will win!" explained Kay G. Fann.

One Step Further
Does your name contain any consonant blends? Which ones?

Missing Digraphs

Directions: Fill in the circle beside the missing digraph in each word.

_wh_ale
- ● wh
- ○ wr
- ○ ch

pea_ch_
- ○ ck
- ○ th
- ● ch

_kn_ife
- ● kn
- ○ ch
- ○ wr

_ch_imp
- ○ ck
- ○ kn
- ● ch

____ell
- ○ ch
- ○ sh
- ○ ck

clo____
- ○ ck
- ○ ch
- ○ kn

____ite
- ○ kn
- ○ wr
- ○ th

fi____
- ○ ch
- ○ sh
- ○ th

____orn
- ○ th
- ○ wr
- ○ ch

One Step Further
Look at the digraphs that are not filled in.
Name words using those digraphs.

Ending Digraphs

Some words end with consonant digraphs. Listen for the ending digraphs in **duck**, **moth**, **dish**, and **branch**.

du**ck**   mo**th**   di**sh**   bran**ch**

Directions: Say the name of each picture. Circle the letters that stand for the ending sound.

ck
th
sh
ch

ck
th
sh
wh

ck
th
sh
ch

ck
th
sh
ch

ck
th
sh
ch

ck
th
sh
ch

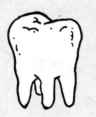
ck
th
sh
ch

ck
th
sh
ch

ck
th
sh
ch

READING

One Step Further

Look at the clock right before you go to sleep. What time does it say?

Silent Letters

Some words have letters you cannot hear at all, such as the **gh** in **night**, the **w** in **wrong**, the **l** in **walk**, the **k** in **knee**, the **b** in **climb**, and the **t** in **listen**.

Directions: Look at the words in the word box. Write the word under its picture. Underline the silent letters.

knife	light	calf	wrench	lamb	eight
wrist	whistle	comb	thumb	knob	knee

_____   _____   _____   _____

_____   _____   _____   _____

_____   _____   _____   _____

One Step Further
Think of other words you know that have a silent letter. What are those words?

READING

A Flying Saucer?

A **discus** is a flat circle made mostly of wood with a metal center and edge that looks a bit like a plate. A men's discus is about nine inches across and weighs a little over four pounds. A women's discus is about two inches smaller and about two pounds lighter. The men's world record throw is 243 feet, but the women's world record is even greater—252 feet!

Directions: Read the word in each discus. Write its silent consonant in the center.

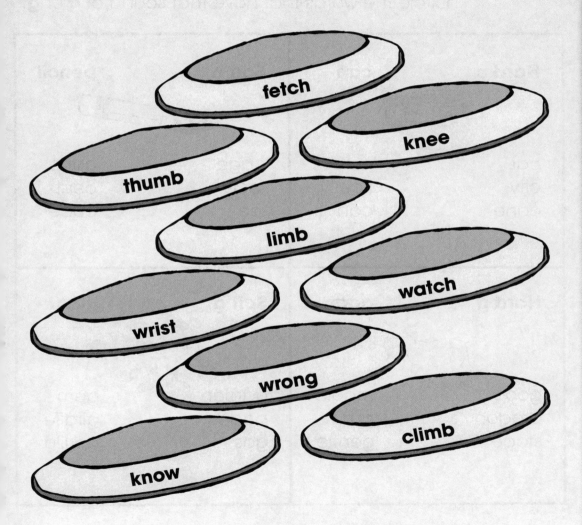

READING

One Step Further
Toss a Frisbee with a friend.
How many catches can you make in a row?

Sounds of c and g

Consonants **c** and **g** each have two sounds. Listen for the soft **c** sound in **pencil**. Listen for the hard **c** sound in **cup**.

Listen for the soft **g** sound in **giant**. Listen for the hard **g** sound in **goat**. **C** and **g** usually have the soft sound when they are followed by **e**, **i**, or **y**.

Directions: Say the name of each picture. Listen for the sound of **c** or **g**. Then, read the words in each list. Circle the words that have that sound of **c** or **g**.

Hard c	cup	Soft c	pencil
car	race	cage	cane
city	rice	face	cent
cone	can	ice	cube

Hard g	goat	Soft g	giant
good	magic	garden	gem
dragon	gum	page	giraffe
stage	gentle	gas	gorilla

One Step Further

List words that contain **c** or **g**.
Write whether those are hard or soft letters.

Hard and Soft c and g

Directions: Circle as many words in each word search as you can find. List them in the correct column.
Hint: The words going up and down have the hard sound, and the words going across and backward have the soft sound.

Hard ⬇   **g**   **Soft ➡**

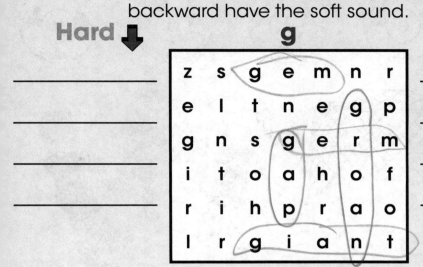

z	s	g	e	m	n	r
e	l	t	n	e	g	p
g	n	s	g	e	r	m
i	t	o	a	h	o	f
r	i	h	p	r	a	o
l	r	g	i	a	n	t

_____   _____
_____   _____
_____   _____
_____   _____

Hint: Two words in the **c** word search go diagonally. They have both a hard and a soft **c** sound.

Hard ⬇   **c**   **Soft ➡**

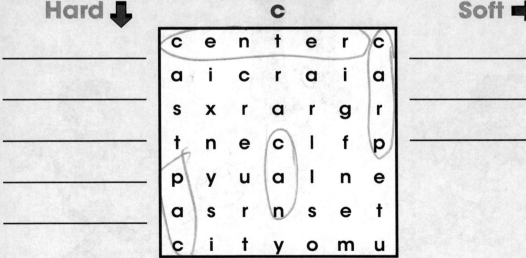

c	e	n	t	e	r	c
a	i	c	r	a	i	a
s	x	r	a	r	g	r
t	n	e	c	l	f	p
p	y	u	a	l	n	e
a	s	r	n	s	e	t
c	i	t	y	o	m	u

_____   _____
_____   _____
_____   _____
_____   _____

Both Hard and Soft

_____   _____

One Step Further
Name a word with a soft **c**, like **center**.
Draw a picture of that word in a circle.

Kick It In!

Directions: Write a vowel to complete each word below.

n____t

p____ss

s____cks

r____n

k____ck

One Step Further

Kick a soccer ball outside. Say a word with a different vowel sound with each kick.

Long Vowels

Long vowel sounds have the same sound as their names. When a **super silent e** comes at the end of a word, you cannot hear it, but it changes the short vowel sound to a long vowel sound.

Example: rope, skate, pie, cute

Directions: Say the names of the pictures. Listen for the long vowel sounds. Write the missing long vowel letter under each picture.

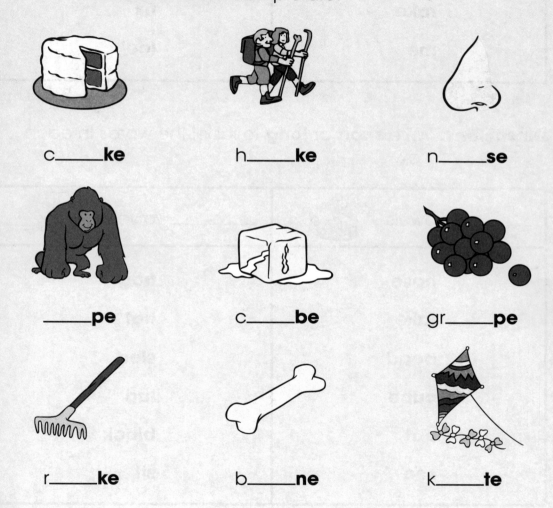

c____**ke**   h____**ke**   n____**se**

____**pe**   c____**be**   gr____**pe**

r____**ke**   b____**ne**   k____**te**

One Step Further
Ask an adult to help you bake a cake. Surprise a friend by giving it to him or her.

Second Grade Essentials

READING

Review

Directions: Read the words in each box. Cross out the word that does **not** belong.

long vowels	short vowels
cube	man
cup	pet
rake	fix
me	ice

Directions: Write **short** or **long** to label the words in each box.

_____ vowels	_____ vowels
hose	frog
take	hot
bead	sled
cube	lap
eat	block
see	sit

One Step Further

Think about the vowels in your first name.
Are they long or short?

Patterns

Directions: Color the spaces with short vowel words **green**.
Color the spaces with long vowel words _____.

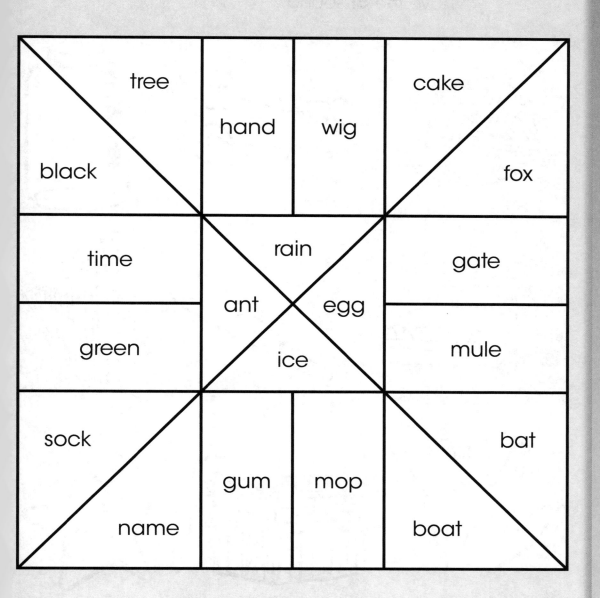

tree

cake

hand   wig

black   fox

time   gate

rain

ant   egg

green   ice   mule

sock   bat

gum   mop

name   boat

READING

One Step Further

What categories could you use to sort the words on this page?

Tricky ar

When **r** follows a vowel, it changes the vowel's sound. Listen for the **ar** sound in **star**.

st**ar**

Directions: Color the pictures whose names have the **ar** sound.

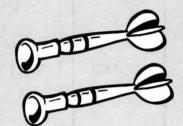

One Step Further

Draw 10 stars. Write a word that starts with the letter **s** on each star.

READING

Write ar or or

Listen for the **or** sound in **horn**.

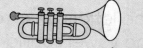
horn

Directions: Write **ar** or **or** to complete each word.

40

th___n   c___t   f___ty

st___k   c___n   h___p

___m   st___   p___ch

One Step Further
Draw a picture of a flower in a jar. Label the parts of the flower, including the thorns.

Second Grade Essentials

READING

Mix and Match

The letters **ur**, **er**, and **ir** all have the same sound. Listen for the vowel sound in **surf**, **fern**, and **girl**.

surf    fern    girl

Directions: Draw a line from each word to the picture it names.

herd

turkey

clerk

thirty

30

purse

bird

One Step Further
Name 10 friends or family members. Then, write them out in ABC order.

READING

Write ur, er, and ir

Directions: Find a word from the box to name each picture. Write it on the line below the picture.

turkey	clerk	dirt	fern	thirty
girl	herd	purple	surf	

_____

_____

_____

_____

_____

_____

_____

_____

30

_____

One Step Further

Draw a turkey. Write a **ur**, **er**, or **ir** word on each of the turkey's feathers.

Vowel Pairs ai and ay

You know that the letters **a__e** usually stand for the long **a** sound. The vowel pairs **ai** and **ay** can stand for the long **a** sound, too. Listen for the long **a** sound in **train** and **hay**.

Directions: Say the name of each picture below. Look at the vowel pair that stands for the long **a** sound. Under each picture, write the words from the box that have the same long **a** vowel pair.

cage	play	pay	gate	stay	skate
mail	chain	snake	snail	gray	tail

 cake    train    hay

_____   _____   _____

_____   _____   _____

_____   _____   _____

_____   _____   _____

One Step Further
Name rhyming words for **cake, train**, and **hay**. How are those words spelled?

Vowel Pairs oa and ow

You know that the letters **o__e** and **oe** usually stand for the long **o** sound. The vowel pairs **oa** and **ow** can stand for the long **o** sound, too. Listen for the long **o** sound in **road** and **snow**.

Directions: Find and circle eight long **o** words. The words may go across or down. Beside each picture, write the words that use the same long **o** vowel pair.

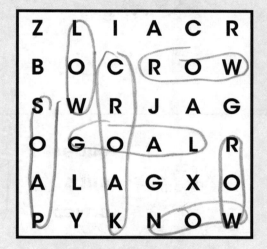

```
Z  L  I  A  C  R
B  O  C  R  O  W
S  W  R  J  A  G
O  G  O  A  L  R
A  L  A  G  X  O
P  Y  K  N  O  W
```

road _____ _____

_____ _____

snow _____ _____

_____ _____

One Step Further
Walk or ride your bike down the road you live on. What do you pass?

Vowel Pair ui

You know that the letters **u__e** and **ue** usually stand for the long **u** sound. The vowel pair **ui** can stand for the long **u** sound, too. Listen for the long **u** sound in **cruise**.

 cruise

Directions: Circle the name of the picture. Then, write the name on the line.

mall
male
mule

sun
Sue
say

fruit
flat
frame

_____

sun
sit
suit

cubes
cubs
caves

Jake
juice
just

_____

fly
flute
fleece

globe
gull
glue

blue
black
ball

_____

One Step Further

Pretend you are on a cruise ship and can sail anywhere in the world. Where would you go?

READING

Vowel Pair ie

You know that the letters **i__e** usually stand for the long **i** sound. The vowel pair **ie** can stand for the long **i** sound, too. Listen for the long **i** sound in **butterflies**.

Directions: Write **i__e** or **ie** to complete each word.

butterfl**ie**s

__ d m __   __ t __   fl __ s __

__ f v __   kn f __   tr __ d __

__ p __   __ l __   k t __

One Step Further

Choose one **i_e** word and one **ie** word.
Draw each picture here.

Vowel Pair ea

Some vowel pairs can stand for more than one sound. The vowel pair **ea** has the sound of long **e** in **team** and short **e** in **head**.

team  head

Directions: Say the name of each picture. Listen for the sound that **ea** stands for. Circle **Long e** or **Short e**. Then, color the pictures whose names have the short **e** sound.

| Long e   Short e | Long e   Short e | Long e   Short e |

 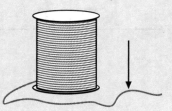 

| Long e   Short e | Long e   Short e | Long e   Short e |

| Long e   Short e | Long e   Short e | Long e   Short e |

One Step Further
Talk about a team that you have been on recently. What was your role on the team?

READING

Vowel Pair oo

Listen for the difference between the sound of the vowel pair **oo** in **moon** and its sound in **book**.

m**oo**n b**oo**k

Directions: Say the name of the picture. Circle the picture of the moon or the book to show the sound of vowel pair **oo**.

READING

One Step Further

What is the best book you've read recently?
What did you like about it?

Y as a Vowel

Y as a vowel can make two sounds. **Y** can make the long sound of **e** or the long sound of **i**.

Directions: Color the spaces:
        purple – **y** sounds like **i**.
        – **y** sounds like **e**.

What is the picture? _____

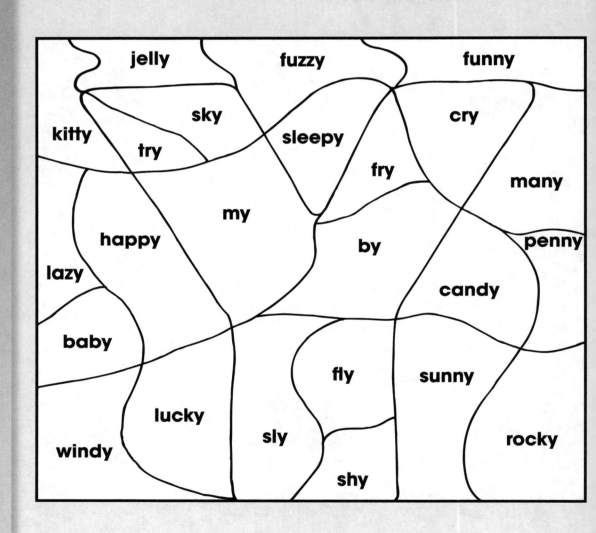

jelly   fuzzy   funny

sky   cry

kitty   sleepy

try   fry

many

my

happy   by

lazy   penny

candy

baby

fly   sunny

lucky

sly   rocky

windy   shy

One Step Further

Write a sentence using as many words on this page as you can.

A Fork in the Road

Directions: Write the words below on the correct "road."

sky	jelly	try	kitty	dry	my
fry	cry	funny	happy	lazy	baby
candy	by	sleepy	many	penny	
sly	fuzzy	shy	fly	why	

_____   _____

_____   _____

_____   _____

_____   _____

_____   _____

_____   _____

_____   _____

_____   _____

_____

_____   _____

Y sounds like long **e**.   **Y** sounds like long **i**.

One Step Further
Draw a road that takes you across a map of
the United States. Label the states you pass.

Second Grade Essentials

Common Nouns

A **common noun** names a person, place, or thing.

Example: The **boy** had several **chores** to do.

Directions: Fill in the circle below each common noun.

1. First, the boy had to feed his puppy.
   ○   ○   ○   ○

2. He got fresh water for his pet.
   ○   ○   ○○

3. Next, the boy poured some dry food into a bowl.
   ○   ○   ○   ○

4. He set the dish on the floor in the kitchen.
   ○   ○   ○   ○

5. Then, he called his dog to come to dinner.
   ○   ○   ○

6. The boy and his dad worked in the garden.
   ○   ○   ○   ○

7. The father turned the dirt with a shovel.
   ○   ○   ○   ○

8. The boy carefully dropped seeds into little holes.
   ○   ○   ○   ○

One Step Further

What are some common nouns that name
things you use each day?

Proper Nouns

A **proper noun** names a specific or certain person, place, or thing. A proper noun always begins with a capital letter.

Example: Becky flew to **St. Louis** in a **Boeing 747**.

Directions: Put a ✔ in front of each proper noun.

_____ 1. uncle   _____ 7. librarian

_____ 2. Aunt Retta   _____ 8. Ms. Small

_____ 3. Forest Park   _____ 9. Doctor Chang

_____ 4. Gateway Arch   _____10. Union Station

_____ 5. Missouri   _____11. Henry Shaw

_____ 6. school   _____12. museum

Directions: Underline the proper nouns.

1. Becky went to visit Uncle Harry.

2. He took her to see the Cardinals play baseball.

3. The game was at Busch Stadium.

4. The St. Louis Cardinals played the Chicago Cubs.

One Step Further

Name proper nouns that are a part of your everyday life, like your school, street, or city.

READING

Singular Nouns

A **singular noun** names one person, place, or thing.

Example: My **mother** unlocked the old **trunk** in the **attic**.

Directions: If the noun is singular, draw a line from it to the trunk. If the noun is **not** singular, draw an **X** on the word.

teddy bear	hammer	picture	sweater
bonnet	letters	seashells	fiddle
kite	ring	feather	books
postcard	crayon	doll	dishes
blocks	hats	bicycle	blanket

One Step Further

What is a singular noun that names something you can find in your bedroom?

Plural Nouns

A **plural noun** names more than one person, place, or thing.

Example: Some **dinosaurs** ate **plants** in **swamps**.

Directions: Underline each plural noun.

1. Large animals lived millions of years ago.

2. Dinosaurs roamed many parts of Earth.

3. Scientists look for fossils.

4. The bones can tell a scientist many things.

5. These bones help tell what the creatures were like.

6. Some had curved claws and whip-like tails.

7. Others had beaks and plates of armor.

8. Some dinosaurs lived on the plains, and others lived in forests.

One Step Further
Write a story about playing sports. What plural nouns did you use?

Second Grade Essentials

READING

Action Verbs

A **verb** is a word that can show action.

Example: I **jump**.   He **kicks**.   He **walked**.

Directions: Underline the verb in each sentence. Write it on the line.

1. Our school plays games on Field Day. _____

2. Juan runs 50 yards. _____

3. Carmen hops in a sack race. _____

4. Paula tosses a ball through a hoop. _____

5. One girl carries a jellybean on a spoon. _____

6. Lola bounces the ball. _____

7. Some boys chase after balloons. _____

8. Mark chooses me for his team. _____

One Step Further

What action verbs do you do each day?
Go outside and run, skip, and hop.

Verbs

Directions: Circle the words in the puzzle. The words go across, down, and diagonally.

```
s w i m k s w u t p a r y
z t p j o m a v o q r e s
y a o n l g l a u g h a z
w s q u m l k w n m l d k
w t x i c l h a n s w e r
r e r g f h e x h i g h a
i c a t c h d y s e e j b
t s v c o l z e c t a c b
e t u s i n g e d f c r y
```

swim   catch    laugh
read   walk   taste
touch   answer   sing
write   see   cry

One Step Further
What did you do yesterday? Write a verb to describe each action you remember.

Linking Verbs

A **linking verb** does not show action. Instead, it links the subject with a word in the predicate. **Am**, **is**, **are**, **was**, and **were** are **linking verbs**.

Example: Many people **are** collectors.
(**Are** connects **people** and **collectors**.)
The collection **was** large.
(**Was** connects **collection** and **large**.)

Directions: Underline the linking verb in each sentence.

1. I am happy.

2. Toy collecting is a nice hobby.

3. Mom and Dad are helpful.

4. The rabbit is beautiful.

5. Itsy and Bitsy are stuffed mice.

6. Monday was special.

7. I was excited.

8. The elephants were gray.

One Step Further
Write several sentences about yourself.
Start each sentence with "I am …"

Irregular Verbs

Verbs that do not add **ed** to show what happened in the past are called **irregular verbs**.

Example: Present   Past
run, runs   ran
fall, falls   fell

Jim **ran** past our house yesterday.
He **fell** over a wagon on the sidewalk.

Directions: Fill in the verbs that tell what happened in the past in the chart. The first one is done for you.

Present	Past
hear, hears	heard
draw, draws	
do, does	
give, gives	
sell, sells	
come, comes	
fly, flies	
build, builds	

One Step Further
Think of something you did yesterday.
Will you do the same thing again today?

Is, Are, and Am

Is, **are**, and **am** are special action words that tell us something is happening now.

Use **am** with I. **Example:** I **am**.
Use **is** to tell about one person or thing. **Example:** He **is**.
Use **are** to tell about more than one. **Example:** We **are**.
Use **are** with **you**. **Example:** You **are**.

Directions: Write **is**, **are**, or **am** in the sentences below.

1. My friends _____ helping me build a tree house.

2. It _____ in my backyard.

3. We _____ using hammers, wood, and nails.

4. It _____ a very hard job.

5. I _____ lucky to have good friends.

One Step Further

Write a sentence about you and two friends.
What action word did you use?

Was and Were

Was and **were** tell us about something that already happened.

Use **was** to tell about one person or thing. **Example:** I **was**, he **was**. Use **were** to tell about more than one person or thing or when using the word **you**. **Example:** We **were**, you **were**.

Directions: Write **was** or **were** in each sentence.

1. Lily _____ eight years old on her birthday.

2. Tim and Steve _____ happy to be at the party.

3. Megan _____ too shy to sing "Happy Birthday."

4. Ben _____ sorry he dropped his cake.

5. All of the children _____ happy to be invited.

One Step Further

Tell a story about something that happened yesterday. What were you doing?

Second Grade Essentials

Go, Going, and Went

We use **go** or **going** to tell about now or later. Sometimes we use **going** with the words **am** or **are**. We use **went** to tell about something that already happened.

Directions: Write **go**, **going**, or **went** in the sentences below.

1. Today, I will _____ to the store.

2. Yesterday, we _____ shopping.

3. I am _____ to take Muffy to the vet.

4. Jan and Steve _____ to the party.

5. They are _____ to have a good day.

One Step Further

Name places you are going today.
Where will you go tomorrow?

Have, Has, and Had

We use **have** and **has** to tell about now. We use **had** to tell about something that already happened.

Directions: Write **has, have,** or **had** in the sentences below.

1. We _____ three cats at home.

2. Ginger _____ brown fur.

3. Bucky and Charlie _____ gray fur.

4. My friend Tom _____ one cat, but it died.

5. Tom _____ a new cat now.

One Step Further

Name something you have. Name something you had yesterday, but not today.

Second Grade Essentials

READING

See, Saw, and Sees

We use **see** or **sees** to tell about now. We use **saw** to tell about something that already happened.

Directions: Write **see**, **sees**, or **saw** in the sentences below.

1. Last night, we _____ the stars.

2. John can _____ the stars from his window.

3. He _____ them every night.

4. Last week, he _____ the Big Dipper.

5. Can you _____ it in the night sky, too?

6. If you _____ it, you would remember it!

7. John _____ it often now.

8. How often do you _____ it?

1 time!!!

One Step Further

Name something interesting you saw yesterday. Tell a story about it.

Eat, Eats, and Ate

We use **eat** or **eats** to tell about now. We use **ate** to tell about what already happened.

Directions: Write **eat**, **eats**, or **ate** in the sentences below.

1. We like to _____ in the lunchroom.

2. Today, my teacher will _____ in a different room.

3. She _____ with the other teachers.

4. Yesterday, we _____ pizza, pears, and peas.

5. Today, we will _____ turkey and potatoes.

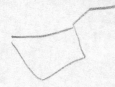

One Step Further
What is your favorite thing to eat?
Name everything you ate yesterday.

Second Grade Essentials

READING

Adjectives

An **adjective** is a word that describes a noun. It tells **how many**, **what kind**, or **which one**.

Example: Yolanda has a **tasty** lunch.

Directions: Color each space that has an adjective. Do not color the other spaces.

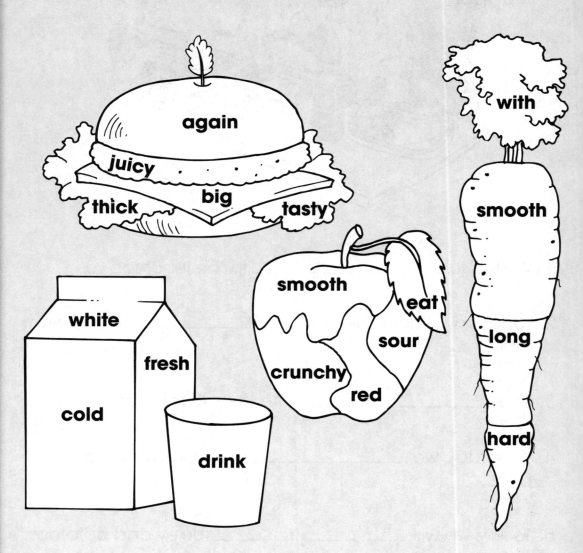

again

juicy

big

thick

tasty

white

fresh

cold

drink

smooth

eat

sour

crunchy

red

with

smooth

long

hard

One Step Further

What adjectives would you use to describe your school? Name as many as you can.

Better Sentences

Directions: Describing words like adjectives can make a better sentence. Write a word on each line to make the sentences more interesting. Draw pictures of your sentences.

1. The skater won a medal.

   The _____ skater won a _____ medal.

2. The jewels were in the safe.

   The _____ jewels were in the _____ safe.

3. The airplane flew through the storm.

   The _____ airplane flew through the _____ storm.

4. A firefighter rushed into the house.

   A _____ firefighter rushed into the _____ house.

5. The detective hid behind the tree.

   The _____ detective hid behind the _____ tree.

1.	2.

3.	4.	5.

One Step Further

Write a sentence. Then, make it better by adding adjectives to the sentence.

Second Grade Essentials

READING

Compound Words

Directions: Read the sentences. Fill in the blank with a compound word from the box.

raincoat	bedroom	lunchbox	hallway	sandbox

1. A box with sand is a

_____.

2. The way through a hall is a

_____.

3. A box for lunch is a

_____.

4. A coat for the rain is a

_____.

5. A room with a bed is a

_____.

One Step Further
What is your favorite food to pack in
your lunchbox?

Word Magic

Maggie Magician announced, "One plus one equals one!"
The audience giggled. So, Maggie put two words into a hat
and waved her magic wand. When she reached into the
hat, Maggie pulled out one word and a picture.
"See," said Maggie, "I was right!"

Directions: Use the word box to help you write a
compound word for each picture below.

ball	rain	shirt	fish	book	basket
bow	box	light	cup	tail	worm
door	star	bell	shoe	foot	
lace	stool	sun	mail	cake	

bookworm   sunshine

cupcack   doorbey

basketball   football

rainbow   tailshin   starfish

One Step Further
Go outside and play a game of basketball
with a friend.

Compound Fun

Directions: Match each word in the box with a word in the puzzle to make a new word.

cake	shine	knob	room
port	shore	ball	fish

1. | s | e | a | | | | |

2. | a | i | r | | | |

3. | p | a | n | | | |

4. | s | u | n | | | | |

5. | d | o | o | r | | | |

6. | b | a | t | h | | | |

7. | f | o | o | t | | | |

8. | g | o | l | d | | | |

One Step Further
Make up silly new compound words like **fishball**. Write definitions for your words.

Tasty Compounds

Directions: Circle the words in the puzzle. The words go across, down, and diagonally.

```
p e p p e r m i n t x y a
o g g r a p e f r u i t z
p t u j k n s e a f o o d
c v p l s q c u p c a k e
o w e m o r o a t m e a l
r i a n b r e a k f a s t
n g n p b l u e b e r r y
f h u e f r u i t c a k e
w a t e r m e l o n b d c
```

watermelon	fruitcake	peppermint
popcorn	cupcake	blueberry
pancake	breakfast	grapefruit
oatmeal	peanut	seafood

One Step Further
Plan a special meal for your mom or dad.
Write the menu.

Contractions

A **contraction** is a word made up of two words joined together with one or more letters left out. An **apostrophe** is used in place of the missing letters.

Example: I am—**I'm**
do not—**don't**
that is—**that's**

Directions: Draw a line to match each contraction to the words from which it was made. The first one is done for you.

1. he's	we are	6. they'll	are not
2. we're	cannot	7. aren't	they will
3. can't	he is	8. I've	you have
4. I'll	she is	9. you've	will not
5. she's	I will	10. won't	I have

One Step Further

Write more contractions you know.
How often do you use contractions?

Contractions

Contractions are a short way to write two words, such as **isn't**, **I've**, and **weren't**.

Example: it is—**it's**

Directions: Draw a line from each word pair to its contraction.

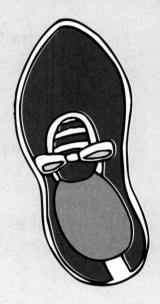 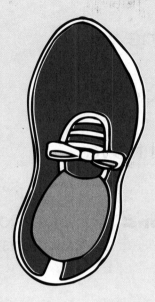

I am	she's
it is	they're
you are	we're
we are	he's
they are	I'm
she is	it's
he is	you're

One Step Further

Write a sentence using one of the contractions on this page.

Contractions

Directions: Match the words with their contractions.

would not	I've
was not	he'll
he will	wouldn't
could not	wasn't
I have	couldn't

Directions: Make the words at the end of each line into contractions to complete the sentences.

1. He _____ know the answer.   **did not**

2. _____ a long way home.   **It is**

3. _____ my house.   **Here is**

4. _____ not going to school today. **We are**

One Step Further
Write a story. How many contractions can you use?

Something Is Missing!

Directions: Write the correct contraction for each set of
words. Then, circle the letter that was left out
when the contraction was made.

| doesn't | it's | didn't | who's | he's |
| don't | aren't | she's | that's | isn't |

1. he is _____

2. are not _____

3. do not _____

4. who is _____

5. is not _____

6. did not _____

7. it is _____

8. she is _____

9. does not _____

10. that is _____

Directions: Write the missing contraction on the line.

1. _____ on her way to school.

2. There _____ enough time to finish the story.

3. Do you think _____ too long?

4. We _____ going to the party.

5. Donna _____ like the movie.

6. _____ going to try for a part in the play?

7. Bob said _____ going to run in the big race.

8. They _____ know how to bake a cake.

9. Tom _____ want to go skating on Saturday.

10. Look, _____ where they found the lost watch.

One Step Further
Write a letter to a friend.
Use as many contractions as you can.

READING

Prefixes

Directions: Change the meaning of the sentences by adding prefixes to the **bold** words.

The boy was **lucky** because he guessed the answer **correctly**.

The boy was (un) _____ because

he guessed the answer (in) _____.

When Mary **behaved**, she felt **happy**.

When Mary (mis) _____, she felt

(un) _____.

Mike wore his jacket **buttoned** because the dance was **formal**.

Mike wore his jacket (un) _____

because the dance was (in) _____.

One Step Further
Tell a story about a time you misbehaved.
What happened after you misbehaved?

Prefixes: The Three Rs

Prefixes are syllables added to the beginning of words that change their meaning. The prefix **re** means "again."

Directions: Read the story. Then, follow the instructions.

Kim wants to find ways she can save Earth. She studies the "three Rs"—reduce, reuse, and recycle. **Reduce** means to make less. Both **reuse** and **recycle** mean to use again.

Add **re** to the beginning of each word below. Use the new words to complete the sentences.

_____ build   _____ write   _____ tell

_____ read   _____ fill   _____ run

1. The race was a tie, so Dawn and Kathy had to

   _____ it.

2. The block wall fell down, so Simon had to

   _____ it.

3. The water bottle was empty, so Luna had to

   _____ it.

4. Javier wrote a good story, but he wanted to

   _____ it to make it better.

5. The teacher told a story, and the students had to

   _____ it.

6. Toni didn't understand the directions, so she had to

   _____ them.

One Step Further

Do you recycle? Name ways you can reuse different objects.

Second Grade Essentials

Suffixes

A **suffix** is a syllable that is added at the end of a word to change its meaning.

Directions: Add the suffixes to the root words to make new words. Use your new words to complete the sentences.

help + ful = _____

build + er = _____

talk + ed = _____

love + ly = _____

loud + er = _____

_____

1. My mother _____ to my teacher about my homework.

2. The radio was _____ than the television.

3. Sally is always _____ to her mother.

4. A _____ put a new garage on our house.

5. The flowers are _____.

One Step Further

Describe ways you have been helpful to your friends and family.

Suffixes

Directions: Write a word from the word box next to its root word.

coming	visited	running	carried	swimming
lived	hurried	rained	sitting	racing

run _____   come _____

live _____   carry _____

hurry _____   race _____

swim _____   rain _____

visit _____   sit _____

Directions: Write a word from the word box to finish each sentence.

1. I _____ my grandmother during vacation.

2. Mary went _____ at the lake with her cousin.

3. Jim _____ the heavy package for his mother.

4. It _____ and stormed all weekend.

5. Cars go very fast when they are _____.

One Step Further

Write a sentence about something that happened yesterday. Use the suffix **ed**.

READING

Use the Clues

Context clues can help you figure out words you do not know. Read the words around the new word. Think of a word that makes sense.

Kate swam in a _____?_____.

Did Kate swim in a cake or a lake? The word **swim** is a context clue.

Directions: Kate wrote this letter from camp. Read the letter. Use context clues to write the missing words from the word box. What clues did you use?

lake	pancakes	six	forest

Dear Mom and Dad,

  I woke up at _____ o'clock and got

dressed. My friends and I ate _____ for

breakfast. We went hiking in the _____.

Then, we went swimming in the _____.
Camp is fun!

                                        Love, Kate

One Step Further
Write a letter to a friend about everything you did today.

Context Clues in Action

Directions: Read the story. Use context clues to figure out the meanings of the **bold** words. Draw a line from the word to its meaning. The first one is done for you.

Jack has a plan. He wants to take his parents out to lunch to show that he **appreciates** all the nice things they do for him. His sister Jessica will go, too, so she won't feel left out. Jack is **thrifty**. He saves the **allowance** he earns for doing **chores** around the house. So far, Jack has saved 10 dollars. He needs only five dollars more. He is excited about paying the check himself. He will feel like an **adult**.

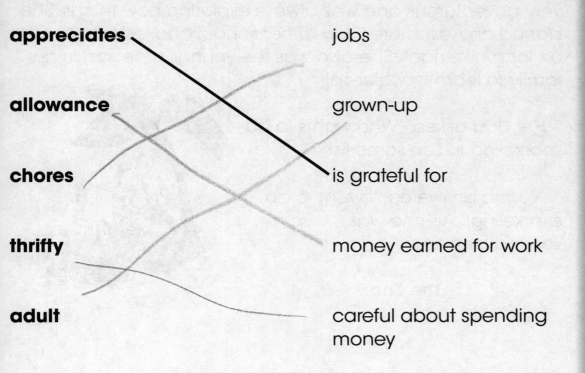

appreciates   jobs

allowance   grown-up

chores   is grateful for

thrifty   money earned for work

adult   careful about spending money

One Step Further

Do something to show that you appreciate a friend or family member.

What Is a Character?

A **character** is the person, animal, or object that a story is about. You cannot have a story without a character.

Characters are usually people, but sometimes they can be animals, aliens, or even objects that come to life. You can have many characters in a story.

Directions: Read the story below, and then answer the questions about character on the next page.

Adventurous Alenna!

Alenna was seven years old and lived on a tropical island. She had long, blond hair and sea-green eyes. Alenna was very adventurous and was always exploring new things. She started an Adventure Club at her school and led her friends on long bike rides. She also was the youngest person in her family to learn to water-ski!

Her dad asked, "Who wants to go snorkeling to see some fish?"

Alenna answered, "I want to go snorkeling!" Alenna was very adventurous.

The End

One Step Further
Who or what is the main character in your favorite book?

Character

First, authors must decide who their main character is going to be. Next, they decide what their main character looks like. Then, they reveal the character's personality by:

what the character does
what the character says

Directions: Answer the questions about the story you just read.

Who is the main character in "Adventurous Alenna!"?

_____

What does Alenna look like? Describe her appearance on the line below:

_____

Give two examples of what Alenna **does** that show that she is adventurous:

1. _____

2. _____

Give an example of what Alenna **says** that reveals she

is adventurous. _____

_____

One Step Further
Create your own character.
What does he or she look like?

Setting — Place

Every story has a **setting**. The setting is the **place** where the story happens. Think of a place that you know well. It could be your room, your kitchen, your backyard, your classroom, or an imaginary place.

Directions: Brainstorm some words and ideas about that place. Think about what you see, hear, smell, taste, or feel in that place.

Brainstorm your ideas for a setting below:

see
hear
smell
taste
touch

_____

_____

_____

_____

_____

_____

_____

_____

Where are we? _____

One Step Further

With a friend, brainstorm ideas for a play.
Act out your play for your family members.

The **setting** is the **place** where the story happens. The setting is also the **time** in which the story happens. A reader needs to know **when** the story is happening. Does it take place at night? On a sunny day? In the future? During the winter?

Time can be:

time of   a holiday   a season   a time in   a time
day   of the year   the future   in history

Directions: Read the following story. Then, answer the questions.

Knock, Knock!

One windy fall night there was a knock at the door. "Who is it?" I asked.

"It's your dog, Max. Please let me in," Max said.

"Oh, good. I was getting worried about you!" I said. Then, I let Max inside.

I thought to myself how glad I was that scientists had invented voice boxes for dogs. How did people in the olden days ever know when to let their dogs inside if their dogs couldn't talk? The Doggie Voice Box is such a wonderful invention. I'm so happy that I live in the year 2090!

What time of day is it? _____

What season is it?_____

What year does this story take place?_____

One Step Further
Brainstorm ideas for a story.
What is the setting of your story?

Tooth Tales

Directions: Read the following information about your teeth.

Did you know that your teeth are made of enamel? Enamel is the hardest material in your entire body. It makes your teeth strong.

There are four different types of teeth in your mouth. Your front four teeth on the top and front four teeth on the bottom are called **incisors**. Ouch! They are sharp teeth used for biting (for biting food that is, not for biting your brother!).

You have two very pointy teeth on the top and two on the bottom called **canines**. They are used for foods that are hard to chew.

In the very back of your mouth, you have 12 wide teeth called **molars**. They are used for grinding food. (These are worth a lot to the Tooth Fairy!)

Finally, you have eight teeth called **bicuspids** for crushing food.

Adults have 32 permanent teeth! That's a lot of teeth, so keep smiling!

One Step Further

Teeth are important for a healthy smile.
What do you do to take care of your teeth?

Tooth Tales

Directions: Answer the questions using information from the article about your teeth.

What are your teeth made of? _____
Highlight where you found the answer.

What is the hardest material in your body? _____
Highlight where you found the answer.

How many different types of teeth are in your mouth? _____
Highlight where you found the answer.

What are your four very pointy teeth called? _____
Highlight where you found the answer.

How many teeth do adults have? _____
Highlight where you found the answer.

What teeth are used for biting? _____
Highlight where you found the answer.

How many molars do people have? _____
Highlight where you found the answer.

READING

One Step Further
How many teeth do you have?
How many teeth have you lost?

Hermit Crabs

Directions: Read about hermit crabs. Use what you learn to finish the sentences.

The hermit crab lives in a shell in or near the ocean. It does not make its own shell. It moves into a shell left by another sea animal. As the hermit crab grows, it gets too big for its shell. It will hunt for a new shell. It will feel the new shell with its claw. If the shell feels just right, the crab will leave its old shell and move into the bigger one. It might even take a shell away from another hermit crab.

1. This story is mostly about the _____.

2. The hermit crab lives _____.

3. When it gets too big for its shell, it will _____

_____

4. The crab will feel the shell with its _____.

5. It might take a shell away from _____

_____

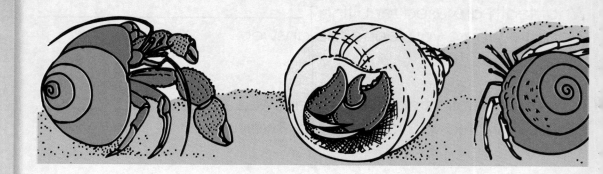

One Step Further
Do you think a hermit crab would make a good pet? Why or why not?

Directions: Read the facts below. Then, read each sentence below. If it is true, put a **T** on the line. If it is false, put an **F** on the line.

The Statue of Liberty is a symbol of the United States. It stands for freedom. It is the tallest statue in the United States.

The statue is of a woman wearing a robe. She is holding a torch in her right hand. She is holding a book in her left hand. She is wearing a crown. The Statue of Liberty was a gift from the country of France.

Each year, people come from all over the world to visit the statue. Not only do they look at it, they can also go inside the statue. At one time, visitors could go all the way up into the arm. In 1916, the arm was closed to visitors because it was too dangerous. The Statue of Liberty is located on an island in New York Harbor.

_____ 1. The Statue of Liberty is a symbol of the United States.

_____ 2. People cannot go inside the statue.

_____ 3. The statue was a gift from Mexico.

_____ 4. People used to be able to climb up into the statue's arm.

_____ 5. It is a very short statue.

One Step Further

Look up another United States landmark. Why is that landmark important?

Sticklebacks

Directions: Read about the stickleback fish. Use the article to help pick the correct answers to fill in the blanks. Circle the correct answer.

Sticklebacks are small fish. They have small spines along their backs. The spines keep other fish from trying to swallow them.

Stickleback fish are odd because the male builds the nest for the eggs. He makes the nest out of water plants and sticks. He makes it in the shape of a barrel and glues it together. He uses a thread-like material from his body to glue the nest together.

When the nest is ready, the mother fish comes. She lays her eggs and goes away. The father stays by the nest and guards the eggs. After the eggs hatch, he stays with the baby fish for a few days. If other sea animals try to eat the baby sticklebacks, he will fight them. He keeps the baby fish safe until they can care for themselves.

1. The story is mostly about _____.

   spines   enemy sea   stickleback fish
                         animals

2. The stickleback is unusual because _____.

   the eggs are   the male builds   the female
   in the nest   a nest   lays eggs

3. The nest is made of _____.

   mud and grass   water plants   string and glue
                         and sticks

4. If an animal tries to eat the baby fish, the stickleback father will _____.

   fight it off   swim away   jump out of
                                                 the water

One Step Further
What is another odd animal that you know of? What makes that animal odd?

Eagles

Directions: Read about eagles. Then, circle the correct ending to each sentence below.

Eagles are large birds. They eat small animals such as mice and rabbits. Eagles make their nests in high places such as the tops of trees. Their nests are made of sticks, weeds, and dirt. Eagles can live in the same nest for many years.

The mother eagle lays one or two eggs each year. When she sits on the eggs, the father eagle brings her food. Baby eagles are called **eaglets**.

1. Eagles are
   large dogs.　　large birds.

2. Eagles eat
   small animals.
   plants and trees.

3. Eagles
   build a nest each year.
   live in the same nest for many years.

4. The mother eagle lays
   one or two eggs.
   three or four eggs.

5. Baby eagles are called
   igloos.　　eaglets.

One Step Further
Write an essay about an animal of your choice. Ask an adult to help you do research.

Second Grade Essentials

Seals

Directions: Read about seals. Then, answer each question using complete sentences.

Seals live in the oceans and on land. They eat different kinds of sea animals, such as fish, shrimp, squid, and krill. They are very good swimmers. They use their flippers to help them move in the water and on the land. They talk to each other by making barking sounds.

1. What do seals eat? _____

_____

2. For what do seals use their flippers? _____

_____

_____

3. Where do seals live? _____

_____

4. How do seals talk? _____

_____

One Step Further
Where do you think you would be most likely to see a seal? Have you seen a seal?

READING

Math

MATH

So Many Vegetables

Directions: Count the number of each vegetable in the picture. Write the number in the correct box.

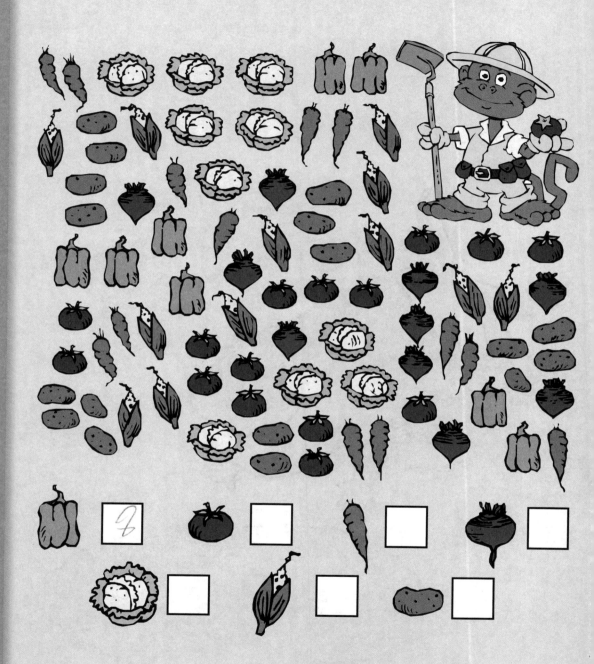

One Step Further

Name your favorite vegetable. Name your favorite fruit. Which do you like better?

Critter Count

Directions: Count by **2**s, **5**s, and **10**s to find the "critter count."

Each worm = 2. Count by **2**s to find the total.

= _____

= _____

Each turtle = 5. Count by **5**s to find the total.

= _____

= _____

Each ladybug = 10. Count by **10**s to find the total.

= _____

= _____

MATH

One Step Further
Go outside and look at the ground.
Count the number of critters you see.

Second Grade Essentials

The Manta Ray

Directions: Connect the dots from **10** to **36**. Color the picture.

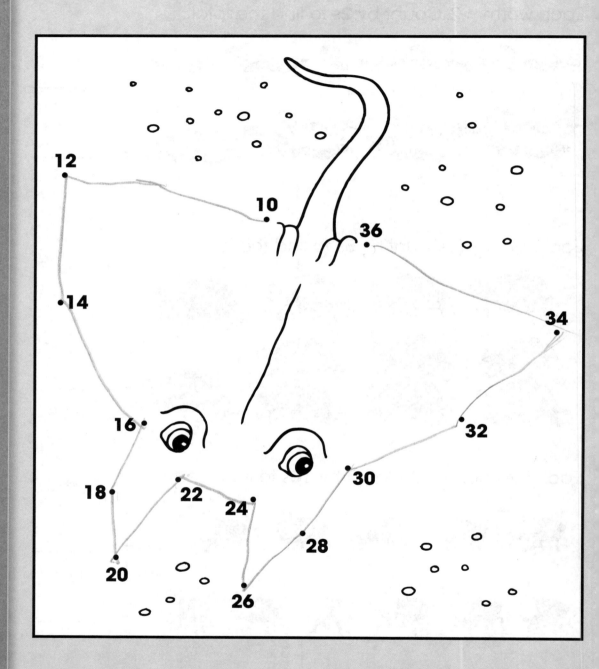

One Step Further

A manta ray is shaped like a triangle. What other animals look like shapes?

Look Out Below!

Directions: Connect the dots from **50** to **88**. Color the picture.

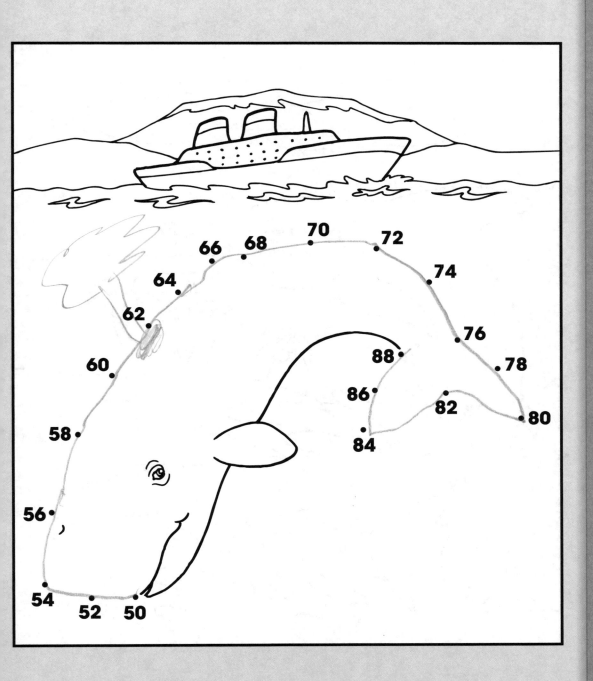

One Step Further

Whales migrate all around the world's oceans. Where would you go if you were a whale?

Second Grade Essentials

Sharpy Swordfish

Directions: Connect the dots from **3** to **27**. Color the picture.

MATH

One Step Further

Be careful! A sword has a sharp point. What other objects are sharp?

What Shark Is This?

Directions: Connect the dots from **24** to **72**. Color the picture.

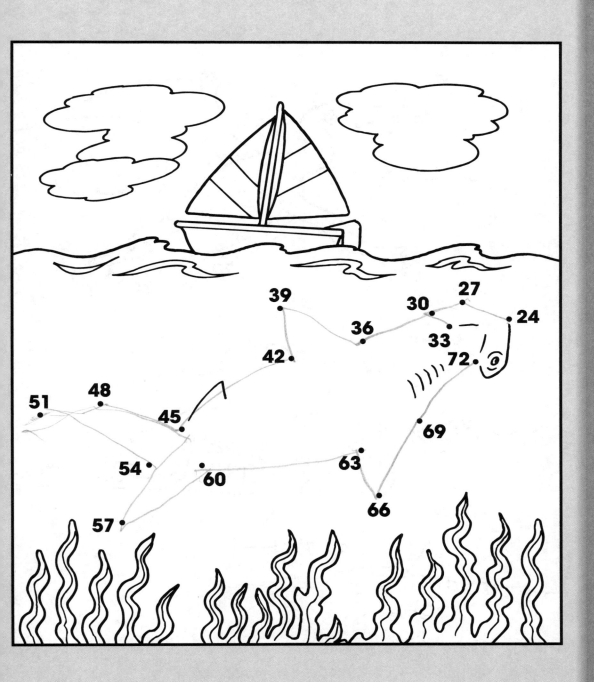

MATH

One Step Further

Name the shark in this picture. With an adult, research two facts about this shark.

Is It a Bird?

Directions: Connect the dots from **0** to **24**. Color the picture.

MATH

One Step Further

Look outside. How many birds can you see right now?

A Crest for a Head

Directions: Connect the dots from **8** to **40**. Color the picture.

MATH

One Step Further

Make some fossils. Press rocks, leaves, and other natural things into clay.

Rapunzel

Directions: Connect the dots from **5** to **70**. Color the picture.

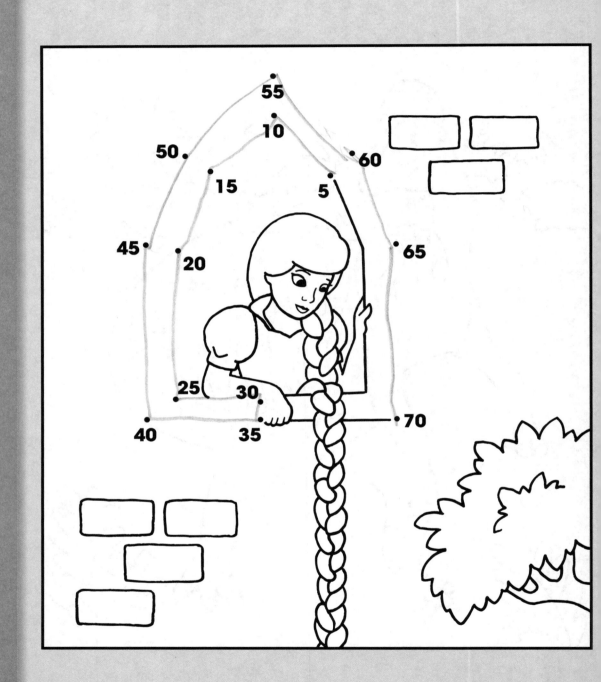

One Step Further

Use yarn or string to make a long braid.
Measure to find out how long it is.

The Princess & the Pea

Directions: Connect the dots from **5** to **100**. Color the picture.

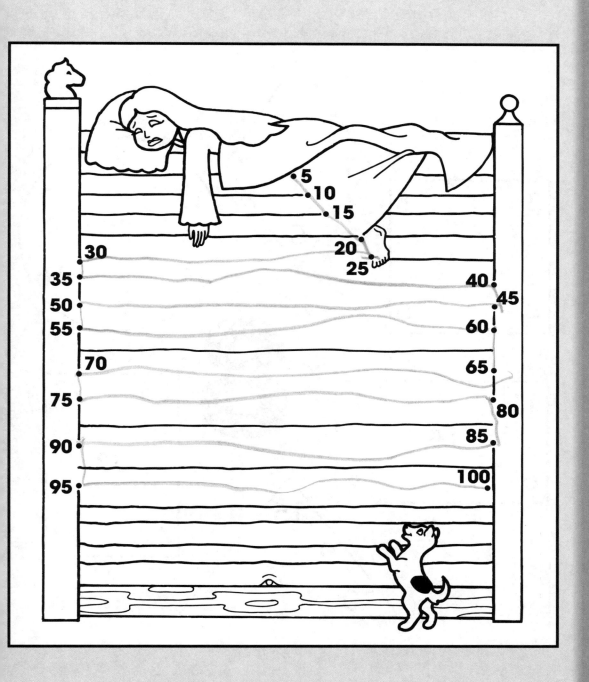

MATH

Second Grade Essentials

One Step Further

Change one thing in a room. Can a friend tell what change you made?

Largest and Smallest

Directions: In each shape, circle the smallest number. Draw a square around the largest number.

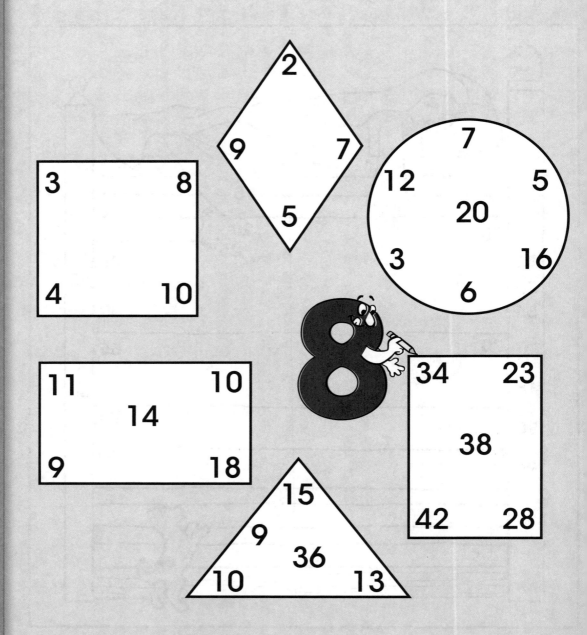

One Step Further

Put several cotton balls into two piles.
Which pile is the largest?

5 > 3
5 is greater than 3.

3 < 5
3 is less than 5.

Directions: Write the missing numbers in the number line.

1	2				6				

Directions: Write **>** or **<**. Use the number line to help you.

5 ◯ 2   1 ◯ 7   1 ◯ 9   8 ◯ 5

3 ◯ 4   9 ◯ 3   8 ◯ 7   2 ◯ 4

6 ◯ 5   5 ◯ 3   5 ◯ 7   3 ◯ 5

7 ◯ 3   7 ◯ 6   2 ◯ 8   4 ◯ 2

MATH

One Step Further
Make a fish face. Hold that face for
10 seconds.

Who Has the Most?

Directions: Circle the correct answer.

1. Traci has 3 🐞s.
   Bob has 4 🐞s.
   Bill has 5 🐞s.
   Who has the most 🐞s?

   Traci   Bob   Bill

2. Pam has 7 🐶s.
   Joe has 5 🐶s.
   Jane has 6 🐶s.
   Who has the most 🐶s?

   Pam   Joe   Jane

3. Jennifer has 23 🐂s.
   Sandy has 19 🐂s.
   Jack has 25 🐂s.
   Who has the most 🐂s?

   Jennifer   Sandy   Jack

4. Ali has 19 🐛s.
   Burt has 18 🐛s.
   Brent has 17 🐛s.
   Who has the most 🐛s?

   Ali   Burt   Brent

5. The boys have 14 🐱s.
   The girls have 16 🐱s.
   The teachers have 17 🐱s.
   Who has the most 🐱s?

   boys   girls   teachers

6. Rose has 12 🐰s.
   Betsy has 11 🐰s.
   Leslie has 13 🐰s.
   Who has the most 🐰s?

   Rose   Betsy   Leslie

One Step Further
Get with a friend and count all your teddy bears. Who has the most?

Who Has the Fewest?

Directions: Circle the correct answer.

1. Pat had 4 ⚽s.
   Charles had 3 ⚽s.
   Andrea had 5 ⚽s.
   Who had the fewest
   number of ⚽s?
   Pat   Charles   Andrea

2. Jeff has 5 🏀s.
   John has 4 🏀s.
   Bill has 6 🏀s.
   Who has the fewest
   number of 🏀s?
   Jeff   John   Bill

3. Jane has 7 ⚾s.
   Susan has 9 ⚾s.
   Fred has 8 ⚾s.
   Who has the fewest
   number of ⚾s?
   Jane   Susan   Fred

4. Charles bought 12 golf balls.
   Rose bought 6 golf balls.
   Dawn bought 24 golf balls.
   Who bought the fewest
   number of golf balls?
   Charles   Rose   Dawn

5. John had 9 🏈s.
   Jack had 8 🏈s.
   Mark had 7 🏈s.
   Who had the fewest
   number of 🏈s?
   John   Jack   Mark

6. Edith bought 12 🎾s.
   Michelle bought 16 🎾s.
   Marty bought 13 🎾s.
   Who bought the fewest
   number of 🎾s?
   Edith   Michelle   Marty

One Step Further
Count the lamps in each room of your home.
Which room has the fewest?

Signs of Gain

Directions: Roll a die. Write the number from the die in the top box. Add to find the sum. Roll again to make each sentence different.

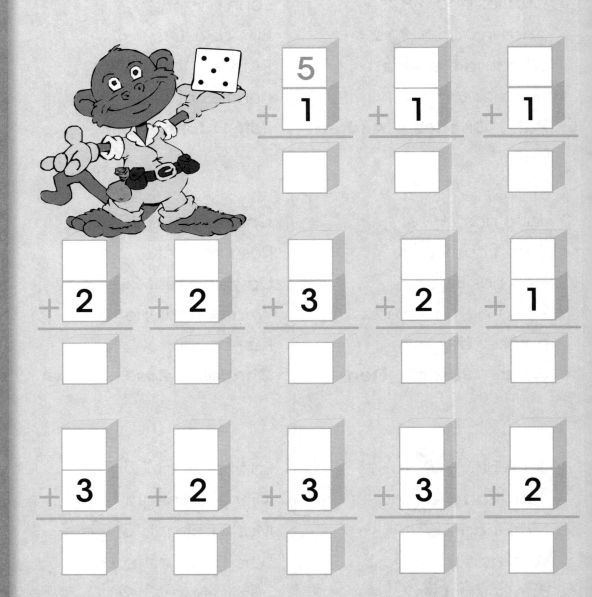

One Step Further

Look at all the numbers you rolled.
Which number did you roll most often?

Counting Up

Directions: Count up to get the sum. Write the missing number in each blank.

$3 + \underline{} = 6$

$4 + \underline{} = 5$

$7 + \underline{} = 9$

$2 + \underline{} = 4$

$3 + \underline{} = 8$

$5 + \underline{} = 5$

$8 + \underline{} = 10$

$7 + \underline{} = 8$

$6 + \underline{} = 9$

$8 + \underline{} = 9$

$4 + \underline{} = 6$

$6 + \underline{} = 6$

$5 + \underline{} = 7$

$4 + \underline{} = 7$

$9 + \underline{} = 10$

$5 + \underline{} = 8$

$7 + \underline{} = 10$

$6 + \underline{} = 8$

MATH

One Step Further

Look around your neighborhood for objects that are tall, like giraffes.

Snorkeling Solutions

Directions: Add the numbers in each mask. Write the sums in the bubbles. Color the bubbles of the four largest sums.

5+6   9+8   5+1   9+7

8+6   7+7   9+9   2+9

10+10   9+5   6+9   7+6

One Step Further

How long can you hold your breath?
Ask an adult to time you.

Add the Apples

Directions: Match the addition sentences with their sums.

8 + 2   15
9 + 6   4
2 + 2   10

1 + 2   11
6 + 7   3
5 + 6   13

3 + 2   10
6 + 8   14
5 + 5   5

6 + 6   12
6 + 3   9
3 + 4   7

6 + 2   8
1 + 1   6
1 + 5   2

7 + 2   15
6 + 9   9
12 + 1   13

10 + 1   14
9 + 5   8
7 + 1   11

MATH

One Step Further

How many apples did you eat this week?
Try to eat more apples next week.

Problem Solving

Directions: Solve each problem.

Example:

 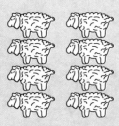

black sheep

white sheep

sheep in all

softballs

baseballs

balls in all

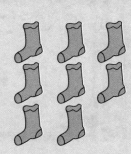

full glasses

empty glasses

glasses in all

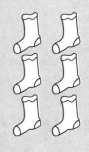

white socks

gray socks

socks in all

One Step Further

Count the different colors of socks in your sock drawer. How many colors are there?

MATH

Food Facts

Directions: Draw pictures to show what happens in each story. Solve the problem.

The monkey holds 2 🍌 s.

He has 8 🍌 s in the jeep.

How many 🍌 s in all? _____

There are 4 🍎 s on the tree.

There are 3 🍎 s on the ground.

How many 🍎 s in all? _____

The monkey picked 2 🍇 s.

There are 6 more 🍇 s left on the vine.

How many 🍇 s in all? _____

One Step Further
Look at the foods on this page.
Which is your favorite? Why?

Second Grade Essentials

MATH

Leaves Leaving the Limb

Directions: Subtract to find the difference. Use the code to color the leaves.

Code: 0 = green   1 = **red**   2 = yellow   3 = **brown**

$$\begin{array}{r} 1 \\ -0 \\ \hline \end{array}$$

$$\begin{array}{r} 5 \\ -2 \\ \hline \end{array}$$

$$\begin{array}{r} 3 \\ -3 \\ \hline \end{array}$$

$$\begin{array}{r} 2 \\ -1 \\ \hline \end{array}$$

$$\begin{array}{r} 3 \\ -1 \\ \hline \end{array}$$

$$\begin{array}{r} 2 \\ -2 \\ \hline \end{array}$$

$$\begin{array}{r} 4 \\ -2 \\ \hline \end{array}$$

$$\begin{array}{r} 5 \\ -3 \\ \hline \end{array}$$

$$\begin{array}{r} 3 \\ -0 \\ \hline \end{array}$$

$$\begin{array}{r} 5 \\ -4 \\ \hline \end{array}$$

$$\begin{array}{r} 1 \\ -1 \\ \hline \end{array}$$

$$\begin{array}{r} 2 \\ -1 \\ \hline \end{array}$$

How many of each color?

 _____   _____   _____   _____

One Step Further
Go outside and find 10 leaves.
How many are green? How many are red?

Looping Differences

Directions: Circle the two numbers next to each other that make the given difference. Find as many as you can in each row.

Difference of 1

| 2 | 3 | 0 | (8 | 7) | 2 | 9 | 10 | 6 | 5 | 1 | 4 | 4 | 3 |

Difference of 1

| 1 | 3 | 4 | 10 | 9 | 7 | 5 | 4 | 2 | 9 | 6 | 2 | 1 | 7 |

Difference of 2

| 4 | 2 | 6 | 3 | 8 | 7 | 5 | 9 | 4 | 3 | 5 | 9 | 7 | 2 |

Difference of 3

| 4 | 6 | 3 | 2 | 0 | 7 | 5 | 2 | 10 | 4 | 0 | 8 | 5 | 3 |

MATH

One Step Further
Put three crayons in one pile and five crayons in another. What is the difference?

Second Grade Essentials

Subtraction Facts

Directions: Subtract.

Example:

$$13 - 5 = 8$$

$$14 - 9$$

$$14 - 8$$

$$13 - 4$$

Directions: Subtract.

12 − 7	10 − 2	13 − 4	14 − 9	11 − 8	14 − 5
14 − 6	12 − 8	13 − 5	10 − 6	13 − 6	13 − 7
11 − 6	13 − 9	14 − 8	12 − 3	14 − 7	13 − 8

One Step Further
Count the basketballs in your school.
Count the soccer balls.

Subtraction Facts

Directions: Subtract.

Example:

$$\begin{array}{r} 15 \\ -\ 7 \\ \hline 8 \end{array}$$

$$\begin{array}{r} 16 \\ -\ 9 \\ \hline \end{array}$$

$$\begin{array}{r} 17 \\ -\ 8 \\ \hline \end{array}$$

$$\begin{array}{r} 18 \\ -\ 9 \\ \hline \end{array}$$

Directions: Subtract.

| $\begin{array}{r} 18 \\ -\ 9 \\ \hline \end{array}$ | $\begin{array}{r} 13 \\ -\ 5 \\ \hline \end{array}$ | $\begin{array}{r} 16 \\ -\ 8 \\ \hline \end{array}$ | $\begin{array}{r} 17 \\ -\ 9 \\ \hline \end{array}$ | $\begin{array}{r} 14 \\ -\ 6 \\ \hline \end{array}$ | $\begin{array}{r} 13 \\ -\ 9 \\ \hline \end{array}$ |

| $\begin{array}{r} 17 \\ -\ 8 \\ \hline \end{array}$ | $\begin{array}{r} 15 \\ -\ 9 \\ \hline \end{array}$ | $\begin{array}{r} 14 \\ -\ 5 \\ \hline \end{array}$ | $\begin{array}{r} 13 \\ -\ 6 \\ \hline \end{array}$ | $\begin{array}{r} 16 \\ -\ 7 \\ \hline \end{array}$ | $\begin{array}{r} 12 \\ -\ 4 \\ \hline \end{array}$ |

| $\begin{array}{r} 14 \\ -\ 7 \\ \hline \end{array}$ | $\begin{array}{r} 15 \\ -\ 8 \\ \hline \end{array}$ | $\begin{array}{r} 16 \\ -\ 9 \\ \hline \end{array}$ | $\begin{array}{r} 12 \\ -\ 7 \\ \hline \end{array}$ | $\begin{array}{r} 15 \\ -\ 7 \\ \hline \end{array}$ | $\begin{array}{r} 13 \\ -\ 4 \\ \hline \end{array}$ |

One Step Further
How many pencils can you find in your desk at school?

MATH

"Grrreat" Picture

Directions: Subtract. Write the answer in the space. Then, color the spaces according to the answers.

1 = **white**   4 = **green**   7 = **pink**   10 = **red**
2 = **purple**   5 = yellow   8 = **gray**
3 = **black**   6 = **blue**   9 = **orange**

MATH

One Step Further
Name a book you've read or movie you've seen about animals.

Swamp Stories

Directions: Read the story. Subtract to find the difference. Write the number in the box.

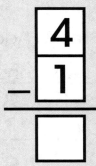

$$\begin{array}{r} 4 \\ -\ 1 \\ \hline \end{array}$$

Four alligators were in the water. One got out.
How many alligators were left in the water?

$$\begin{array}{r} 6 \\ -\ 2 \\ \hline \end{array}$$

Six frogs were sitting on lily pads. Two hopped away.
How many frogs were left on the lily pads?

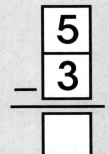

$$\begin{array}{r} 5 \\ -\ 3 \\ \hline \end{array}$$

Five ducks were in the water. Three flew away.
How many ducks were left in the water?

One Step Further

Sit on a couch with two friends. If one friend stands up, how many are still sitting?

MATH

Second Grade Essentials

Two-Digit Addition

Directions: Study the example. Follow the steps to add.

Example:
$$33$$
$$+41$$

Step 1: Add the ones. **Step 2:** Add the tens.

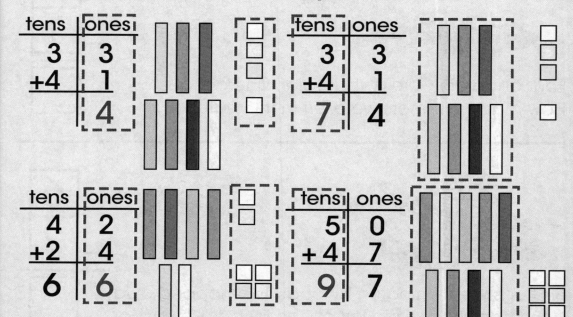

tens	ones
3	3
+4	1
	4

tens	ones
3	3
+4	1
7	4

tens	ones
4	2
+2	4
6	6

tens	ones
5	0
+4	7
9	7

$$24 \quad 15 \quad 38 \quad 11 \quad 37 \quad 72$$
$$+62 \quad +23 \quad +61 \quad +26 \quad +42 \quad +11$$

$$25 \quad 62 \quad 32 \quad 25 \quad 82 \quad 91$$
$$+42 \quad +14 \quad +44 \quad +13 \quad + 6 \quad + 5$$

One Step Further

Ask two adults how old they are.
Add their ages together.

Picture This

Directions: Add the ones, then the tens in each problem.
Then, write the sum in the blank.

Example:

2 tens and 6 ones
+ 1 ten and 3 ones

3 tens and 9 ones = 39

1 ten and 4 ones
+ 3 tens and 3 ones

___ tens and ___ ones = ___

2 tens and 5 ones
+ 2 tens and 3 ones

___ tens and ___ ones = ___

1 ten and 6 ones
+ 5 tens and 1 one

___ tens and ___ ones = ___

1 ten and 3 ones
+ 1 ten and 1 one

___ tens and ___ ones = ___

MATH

One Step Further
Draw a picture of a fish.
Draw 10 bubbles around the fish.

Two-Digit Addition: Regrouping

Addition is "putting together" or adding two or more numbers to find the sum. Regrouping is using **ten ones** to form **one ten**, **ten tens** to form **one 100**, **fifteen ones** to form **one ten** and **five ones**, and so on.

Directions: Study the examples. Follow the steps to add.

Example:
$$14 + 8$$

Step 1:
Add the ones.

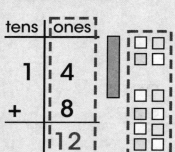

Step 2:
Regroup the tens.

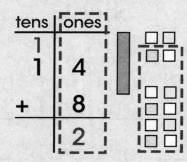

Step 3:
Add the tens.

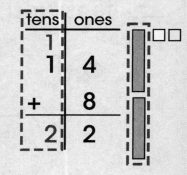

28 +17	32 +38	54 +25	19 +55	44 +48	25 +64

One Step Further

Draw circles for 20 seconds. Then, draw circles for 10 seconds. How many circles did you draw?

Second Grade Essentials

Two-Digit Addition

Directions:

Add the ones.   Rename 11 as 10 + 1.   Add the tens.

```
  38        8              1            1
+43       +3            38           38
                       +43          +43
         11 or 10 + 1 → 1            81
```

Directions: Add.

Example:

```
  17        26        47        68        37
+34       +47       +35       +24       +28
  51
```

```
  29        58        69        78        19
+48       +27       +17       +13       +44
```

```
  55        27        39        57        38
+28       +35       +52       +27       +36
```

```
  49        65        23        64        46
+43       +18       +18       +18       +39
```

MATH

One Step Further
How many states are there? Add that
number to your age. What is the total?

Two-Digit Addition

Directions: Add the total points scored in each game.
Remember to add **ones** first and **tens** second.

Example:

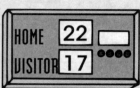 Total ____39____

Total _____

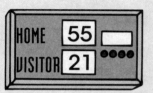

Total _____

Total _____

Total _____

Total _____

Total _____

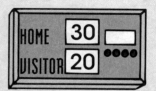

Total _____

Total _____

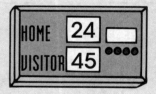

Total _____

One Step Further

What was the score of your favorite team's
last game? Add the numbers together.

Two-Digit Addition: Regrouping

Directions: Add the total points scored in the game. Remember to add the ones, regroup, and then add the tens.

Example:

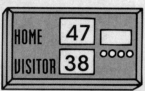

Total ____85____

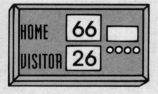   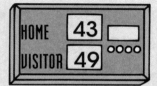   (HOME 57 / VISITOR 34)

Total _____   Total _____   Total _____

(HOME 29 / VISITOR 22)      

Total _____   Total _____   Total _____

(HOME 66 / VISITOR 26)   (HOME 72 / VISITOR 19)   (HOME 54 / VISITOR 26)

Total _____   Total _____   Total _____

MATH

One Step Further
What was the last sports game you watched? Play that sport with a friend.

Problem Solving

Directions: Solve each problem.

Example:

There are 20 men in the plane.

Then, 30 women get in the plane.

How many men and women are in the plane?

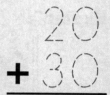

$$\begin{array}{r} 20 \\ + 30 \\ \hline \end{array}$$

_____

Jill buys 10 apples.

Carol buys 20 apples.

How many apples in all?

_____

There are 30 ears of corn in one pile.

There are 50 ears of corn in another pile.

How many ears of corn in all?

_____

Henry cut 40 pieces of wood.

Art cut 20 pieces of wood.

How many pieces of wood were cut?

One Step Further

Name something you collect.

How many items are there in your collection?

Directions: Solve each problem.

Example:

16 boys ride their bikes to school.

18 girls ride their bikes to school.

How many bikes are ridden to school?

$$\begin{array}{r} 16 \\ +\ 18 \\ \hline 34 \end{array}$$

Dad reads 26 pages.

Mike reads 37 pages.

How many pages did Dad and Mike read?

Tiffany counts 46 stars.

Mike counts 39 stars.

How many stars did they count?

Mom has 29 golf balls.

Dad has 43 golf balls.

How many golf balls do they have?

MATH

One Step Further
What is your favorite book?
How many pages is it?

Two-Digit Subtraction

Directions: Look at the example. Follow the steps to subtract.

Example:

$$\begin{array}{r} 28 \\ -14 \\ \hline \end{array}$$

Step 1: Subtract the ones.

tens	ones
2	8
-1	4
	4

Step 2: Subtract the tens.

tens	ones
2	8
-1	4
1	4

$$\begin{array}{r} 24 \\ -12 \\ \hline \end{array} \qquad \begin{array}{r} 61 \\ -30 \\ \hline \end{array} \qquad \begin{array}{r} 77 \\ -44 \\ \hline \end{array} \qquad \begin{array}{r} 85 \\ -24 \\ \hline \end{array} \qquad \begin{array}{r} 57 \\ -23 \\ \hline \end{array} \qquad \begin{array}{r} 87 \\ -33 \\ \hline \end{array}$$

$$\begin{array}{r} 84 \\ -30 \\ \hline \end{array} \qquad \begin{array}{r} 98 \\ -16 \\ \hline \end{array} \qquad \begin{array}{r} 74 \\ -32 \\ \hline \end{array} \qquad \begin{array}{r} 58 \\ -38 \\ \hline \end{array} \qquad \begin{array}{r} 82 \\ -40 \\ \hline \end{array} \qquad \begin{array}{r} 98 \\ -36 \\ \hline \end{array}$$

One Step Further

Ask an adult to write more subtraction problems. How fast can you solve them?

MATH

All Aboard

Directions: Count the tens and ones and write the numbers. Then, subtract to solve the problems.

tens	ones
4	2
2	1

tens	ones

tens	ones

tens	ones

tens	ones

tens	ones

MATH

One Step Further

If you could hop on a train and go anywhere, where would you most like to visit?

Cookie Craze!

Directions: Subtract to solve the problems. Circle the answers. Color the cookies with answers greater than 30.

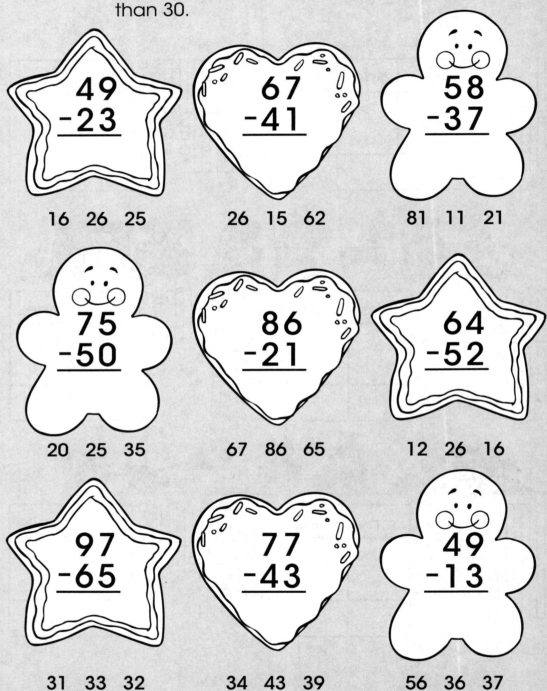

49
-23

16 26 25

67
-41

26 15 62

58
-37

81 11 21

75
-50

20 25 35

86
-21

67 86 65

64
-52

12 26 16

97
-65

31 33 32

77
-43

34 43 39

49
-13

56 36 37

MATH

One Step Further

What is your favorite type of cookie?
Ask an adult to help you bake some.

Prehistoric Problems

Directions: Solve the subtraction problems. Use the code to color the picture.

Code:
25 = **blue**   57 = **green**
31 = yellow   14 = **orange**
21 = **brown**   11 = **red**

```
 47
-22
```

```
 52
-21
```

```
 25
-11
```

```
 62
-31
```

```
 77
-20
```

```
 51
-40
```

```
 98
-41
```

```
 55
-34
```

```
 69
-12
```

MATH

One Step Further
Where might you see dinosaurs today? Write everything you know about dinosaurs.

Two-Digit Subtraction: Regrouping

Subtraction is "taking away" or subtracting one number from another to find the difference. Regrouping is using **one ten** to form **ten ones**, **one 100** to form **ten tens**, and so on.

Directions: Study the examples. Follow the steps to subtract.

Example:
$$37$$
$$-19$$

Step 1:
Regroup.

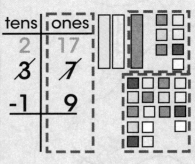

Step 2:
Subtract the ones.

Step 3:
Subtract the tens.

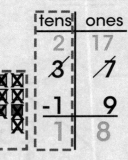
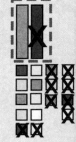

28	46	12	30	52	47
-19	-18	- 8	-12	-25	-35

One Step Further

Ask an adult his or her age. Subtract your age from that number. What did you get?

Two-Digit Subtraction

Directions:

Rename 73 as 6 tens and 13 ones.

```
      6 13
 73    7̶3̶
-48   -48
```

➡

Subtract the ones.

```
  6 13
   7̶3̶
 -48
    5
```

➡

Subtract the tens.

```
  6 13
   7̶3̶
 -48
   25
```

Directions: Subtract.

Example:

```
5 13
 6̶3̶
-48
 15
```

83	74	94	62
-45	-29	-48	-25

45	33	24	86	72
-27	-24	- 8	-37	-48

36	26	43	63	93
-17	-18	-19	-48	-18

82	73	95	57	41
-26	-28	-69	-38	-25

MATH

One Step Further

Write your own set of subtraction problems. See if a friend can answer them correctly.

Subtraction With Regrouping

Directions: Subtract to find the difference. Regroup as needed. Color the spaces with differences of:

10–19 = **red**   50–59 = **brown**   30–39 = **green**

40–49 = yellow   20–29 = **blue**   60–69 = **orange**

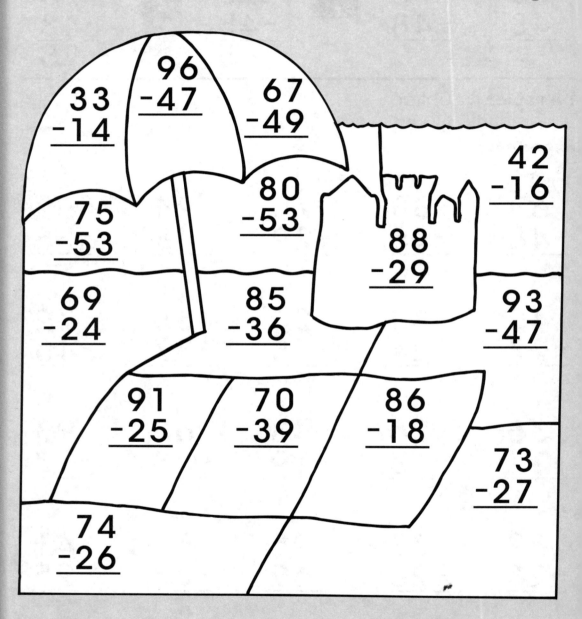

One Step Further

Tell a story about a day at the beach.
What beach would you like to visit?

Go "Fore" It!

Directions: Add or subtract using regrouping.

tens	ones
2	15
~~3~~	~~5~~
-2	7
	8

$$35 + 27$$

$$40 - 16$$

$$56 - 27$$

$$93 - 39$$

$$44 + 28$$

$$42 - 14$$

$$33 + 18$$

$$97 - 48$$

$$73 - 24$$

$$56 - 17$$

$$68 - 49$$

$$49 + 32$$

$$77 - 68$$

$$27 + 19$$

MATH

One Step Further

Go to a driving range with a friend.
See who can hit a golf ball the farthest.

Second Grade Essentials

Monster Math

Directions: Add or subtract using regrouping.

$$\begin{array}{r} 84 \\ -56 \\ \hline \end{array}$$

$$\begin{array}{r} 41 \\ -17 \\ \hline \end{array}$$

$$\begin{array}{r} 52 \\ -28 \\ \hline \end{array}$$

$$\begin{array}{r} 84 \\ -27 \\ \hline \end{array}$$

$$\begin{array}{r} 57 \\ -39 \\ \hline \end{array}$$

$$\begin{array}{r} 72 \\ -19 \\ \hline \end{array}$$

$$\begin{array}{r} 33 \\ -15 \\ \hline \end{array}$$

$$\begin{array}{r} 64 \\ +17 \\ \hline \end{array}$$

$$\begin{array}{r} 36 \\ -19 \\ \hline \end{array}$$

$$\begin{array}{r} 65 \\ -28 \\ \hline \end{array}$$

$$\begin{array}{r} 48 \\ -30 \\ \hline \end{array}$$

$$\begin{array}{r} 33 \\ +18 \\ \hline \end{array}$$

$$\begin{array}{r} 25 \\ +35 \\ \hline \end{array}$$

One Step Further

Make up a scary story about monsters.
Tell it to a friend around a campfire.

Problem Solving

Directions: Solve each problem.

Example:

Dad cooks 23 potatoes.

He uses 19 potatoes in the potato salad.

How many potatoes are left?

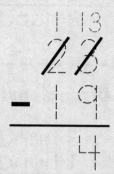

$$\begin{array}{r} {\scriptstyle 1}\;{\scriptstyle 13} \\ \cancel{2}\;\cancel{3} \\ -\; 1\;9 \\ \hline 4 \end{array}$$

Susan draws 32 butterflies.

She colors 15 of them brown.

How many butterflies does she have left to color?

A book has 66 pages.

Pedro reads 39 pages.

How many pages are left to read?

Jerry picks up 34 seashells.

He puts 15 of them in a box.

How many does he have left?

MATH

One Step Further
Draw 14 circles. Color eight red and the rest blue. How many circles are blue?

Adding Hundreds

5 hundreds + 3 hundreds 8 hundreds	5 0 0 + 3 0 0 8 0 0	4 hundreds + 5 hundreds 9 hundreds	4 0 0 + 5 0 0 900

Directions: Add.

3 hundreds + 1 hundreds 4 hundreds	3 0 0 + 1 0 0 400	6 hundreds + 2 hundreds hundreds	6 0 0 + 2 0 0

2 0 0 + 2 0 0	1 0 0 + 7 0 0	6 0 0 + 3 0 0	4 0 0 + 5 0 0

3 0 0 + 4 0 0	8 0 0 + 1 0 0	4 0 0 + 4 0 0	7 0 0 + 2 0 0

5 0 0 + 1 0 0	1 0 0 + 6 0 0	5 0 0 + 2 0 0	3 0 0 + 2 0 0

3 0 0 + 3 0 0	4 0 0 + 2 0 0	3 0 0 + 5 0 0	2 0 0 + 1 0 0

One Step Further

How old would you be in 100 years and in 300 years? Add those numbers together.

MATH

Subtracting Hundreds

8 hundreds	800	6 hundreds	600
- 3 hundreds	- 300	- 2 hundreds	- 200
5 hundreds	500	4 hundreds	400

Directions: Subtract.

9 hundreds	900	3 hundreds	300
- 7 hundreds	- 700	- 1 hundreds	- 100
2 hundreds	200	hundreds	

700	500	900	800
- 300	- 400	- 400	- 500

600	300	500	400
- 500	- 200	- 100	- 200

900	800	600	500
- 100	- 400	- 200	- 300

MATH

One Step Further

Pretend you have $700. If you buy a toy that costs $100, how much will you have left?

Three-Digit Addition

```
  2 4 5              2 4 5              2 4 5
+ 2 5 3            + 2 5 3            + 2 5 3
------- →         -------  →         -------
      8                9 8              4 9 8
```

Directions: Add.

Examples:

```
  7 4 5                    6 2 3
+   2 3                  + 1 5 6
-------                  -------
  7 6 8
```

↑ ↑ ↑ Add the ones.   ↑ ↑ ↑ Add the ones.
      Add the tens.   Add the tens.
      Add the hundreds.   Add the hundreds.

```
  4 1 5          5 6 6          3 7 3          1 6 0
+ 3 4 2        +   3 3        + 2 2 1        + 3 3 4
-------        -------        -------        -------


  8 3 5          6 4 2          2 8 7          7 2 3
+   4 2        + 2 5 1        + 4 1 2        +   4 5
-------        -------        -------        -------


  1 3 3          4 5 4          3 1 4          6 5 4
+ 5 2 2        + 3 2 4        + 6 0 2        + 2 3 5
-------        -------        -------        -------
```

One Step Further

Choose two random three-digit numbers.
Add them together.

Directions:

Subtract the ones.		Subtract the tens.		Subtract the hundreds.

```
  7 4 6          7 4 6          7 4 6
- 4 2 4        - 4 2 4        - 4 2 4
      2            2 2          3 2 2
```

Directions: Subtract.

Examples:

```
  8 7 9
-   4 6
  8 3 3
```
↑ Subtract the ones.
└ Subtract the tens.
└ Subtract the hundreds.

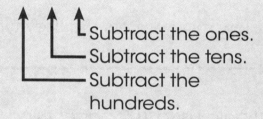

```
  5 8 6
- 1 4 2
```
↑ Subtract the ones.
└ Subtract the tens.
└ Subtract the hundreds.

```
  6 3 5        4 7 8          3 3 8        9 5 7
- 4 2 3      - 2 4 1        -   2 7      - 7 3 4
```

```
  2 9 7        8 4 6          7 6 9        6 5 3
- 1 4 5      - 3 2 5        - 5 1 4      - 1 4 2
```

One Step Further
Choose two random three-digit numbers.
Subtract the smaller one from the bigger one.

Problem Solving

Directions: Solve each problem.

Example:

Ria packed 300 boxes.

Melvin packed 200 boxes.

How many boxes did Ria and Melvin pack?

$$\begin{array}{r} 200 \\ + 300 \\ \hline 500 \end{array}$$

Santo typed 500 letters.

Hale typed 400 letters.

How many letters did they type?

Paula used 100 paper clips.

Milton used 600 paper clips.

How many paper clips did they use?

The grocery store sold 400 red apples.

The grocery store also sold 100 yellow apples.

How many apples did the grocery store sell in all?

One Step Further

Go to the grocery store with an adult. Guess how many apples are being sold.

Problem Solving

Directions: Solve each problem.

Example:

Gene collected 342 rocks.

Lester collected 201 rocks.

How many rocks did they collect?

$$\begin{array}{r} 342 \\ +\ 201 \\ \hline 543 \end{array}$$

Tina jumped the rope 403 times.

Henry jumped the rope 426 times.

How many times did they jump?

There are 210 people wearing blue hats.

There are 432 people wearing red hats.

How many hats in all?

Asta used 135 paper plates.

Clyde used 143 paper plates.

How many paper plates did they use in all?

MATH

One Step Further
Go outside and collect rocks. How many did you find?

Problem Solving

Directions: Solve each problem.

There are 236 boys in school.

There are 250 girls in school.

How many boys and girls are in school?

$$\begin{array}{r} 236 \\ + 250 \\ \hline \end{array}$$

Mary saw 131 cars.

Marvin saw 268 trucks.

How many cars and trucks did they see in all?

Jack has 427 pennies.

Jill has 370 pennies.

How many pennies do they have in all?

There are 582 red apples.

There are 206 yellow apples.

How many apples are there in all?

One Step Further

Look in the parking lot of your school. Count the cars and trucks. Add them together.

Problem Solving

Directions: Solve each problem.

Example:

The grocery store buys 568 cans of beans.

It sells 345 cans of beans.

How many cans of beans are left?

$$\begin{array}{r} 568 \\ -345 \\ \hline 223 \end{array}$$

The cooler holds 732 gallons of milk.

It has 412 gallons of milk in it.

How many more gallons of milk
will it take to fill the cooler?

Ann does 635 push-ups.

Carl does 421 push-ups.

How many more push-ups does Ann do?

Kurt has 386 pennies.

Neal has 32 pennies.

How many more pennies does Kurt have?

MATH

One Step Further
How many push-ups can you do? Practice
every day until you can double your total.

Multiplication

Multiplication is a short way to find the sum of adding the same number a certain amount of times. For example, 7 x 4 = 28 instead of 7 + 7 + 7 + 7 = 28.

Directions: Study the example. Solve the problems.

Example:

3 + 3 + 3 = 9
3 threes = 9
3 x 3 = 9

7 + 7 = _____
2 sevens = _____
2 x 7 = _____

4 + 4 + 4 + 4 = _____
4 fours = _____
4 x _____ = _____

5 + 5 = _____
2 fives = _____
2 x _____ = _____

2 + 2 + 2 + 2 = _____
4 twos = _____
4 x _____ = _____

MATH

One Step Further
Put several small objects into piles of three. Multiply the piles to find the total number.

Multiplication

Multiplication is repeated addition.

Directions: Draw a picture for each problem.
Then, write the missing numbers.

Example: Draw two groups of three apples.

$3 + 3 = 6$
or $2 \times 3 = 6$

Draw three groups of four hearts.

$4 + 4 + 4 =$ _____

or $3 \times$ _____ $=$ _____

Draw two groups of five boxes.

$5 +$ _____ $=$ _____

or $2 \times$ _____ $=$ _____

Draw six groups of two circles.

$2 +$ _____ $+$ _____ $+$ _____ $+$ _____ $+$ _____ $=$ _____

or $6 \times$ _____ $=$ _____

Draw seven groups of three triangles.

$3 +$ _____ $+$ _____ $+$ _____ $+$ _____ $+$ _____ $+$ _____ $=$ _____

or _____ $\times$ _____ $=$ _____

MATH

One Step Further

Draw four groups of three stars.
Ask a friend to multiply them together.

Multiplication

Directions: Study the example. Draw the groups and write the total.

Example:

$$3 \times 2$$
$$2 + 2 + 2 \quad = \quad 6$$

● ●   ● ●   ● ●

3×4

___ + ___ + ___ = ____

2×5

___ + ___ = ____

5×3

___ + ___ + ___ + ___ + ___ = ____

One Step Further

Draw three groups of two trees.
How many trees did you draw?

Multiplication

Directions: Solve the problems.

9 + 9 = ____

7 + 7 = ____

2 nines = ____

2 sevens = ____

2 x 9 = ____

2 x ____ = ____

Multiplication saves time. It's faster than addition!

4 + 4 + 4 + 4 = ____

8 + 8 + 8 + 8 + 8 = ____

____ fours = ____

____ eights = ____

____ x 4 = ____

____ x 8 = ____

5 + 5 + 5 = ____

9 + 9 = ____

6 + 6 + 6 = ____

____ fives = ____

____ nines = ____

____ sixes = ____

____ x 5 = ____

____ x 9 = ____

____ x 6 = ____

3 + 3 = ____

7 + 7 + 7 + 7 = ____

2 + 2 = ____

____ threes = ____

____ sevens = ____

____ twos = ____

____ x 3 = ____

____ x 7 = ____

____ x 2 = ____

MATH

One Step Further

Ask an adult to time how fast you can complete the problems on this page.

Problem Solving

Directions: Tell if you add, subtract, or multiply. Then, write the answers. **Hints:** "In all" means to add. "Left" means to subtract. Groups with the same number in each means to multiply.

Example:

There are six red birds and seven blue birds. How many birds in all?

_____**add**_____ _____**13**_____ birds

The pet store had 25 goldfish, but 10 were sold. How many goldfish are left?

_____ _____ goldfish

There are five cages of bunnies. There are two bunnies in each cage. How many bunnies are there in the store?

_____ _____ bunnies

The store had 18 puppies this morning. It sold seven puppies today. How many puppies are left?

_____ _____ puppies

One Step Further
How many bunnies can you see outside right now? What other animals can you see?

MATH

Problem Solving

Directions: Tell if you add, subtract, or multiply. Then, write the answers.

There were 12 frogs sitting on a log by a pond, but three frogs hopped away. How many frogs were left?

_____ _____ frogs

There are nine flowers growing by the pond. Each flower has two leaves. How many leaves are there?

_____ _____ leaves

A tree had seven squirrels playing in it. Then, eight more came along. How many squirrels are there in all?

_____ _____ squirrels

There were 27 birds living in the trees around the pond, but nine flew away. How many birds are left?

_____ _____ birds

MATH

One Step Further
Find some flowers around your home. How many petals are on the flowers?

Measuring in Inches

Directions: Use a ruler to measure the fish to the nearest inch.

about _____ inches

about _____ inch

about _____ inches

about _____ inch

about _____ inches

about _____ inches

One Step Further

Draw a fish on another piece of paper.
Use the ruler to measure the fish you drew.

Measuring Monkeys

Directions: Use a ruler to measure each rope to the nearest inch. Write the answer in each blank.

One Step Further

Find something in your home that is only one inch long.

Measuring in Centimeters

Directions: Use a centimeter ruler to find the height or the length of the objects below. Write the answer in each blank.

Example:

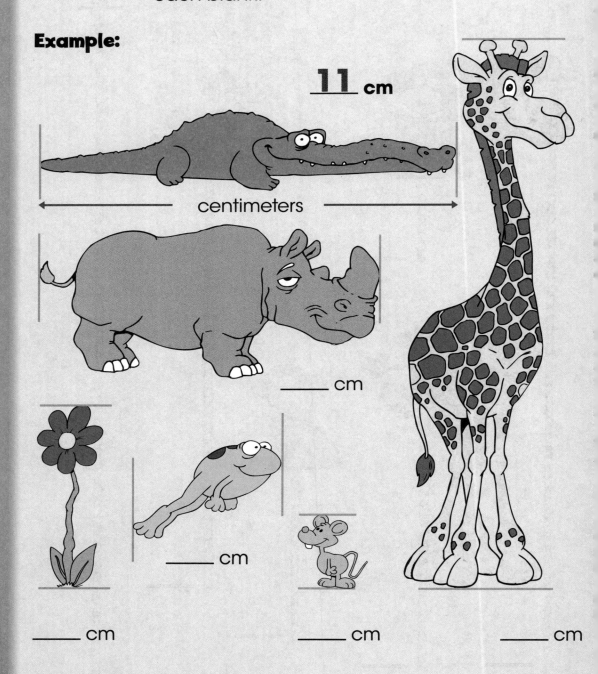

11 cm

centimeters

_____ cm

_____ cm

_____ cm

_____ cm

_____ cm

One Step Further

What is the tallest zoo animal you can think of? What is the longest?

Trip to the Watering Hole

Directions: Use a centimeter ruler to measure the distance each animal has to travel to reach the watering hole. Write the answer in each blank.

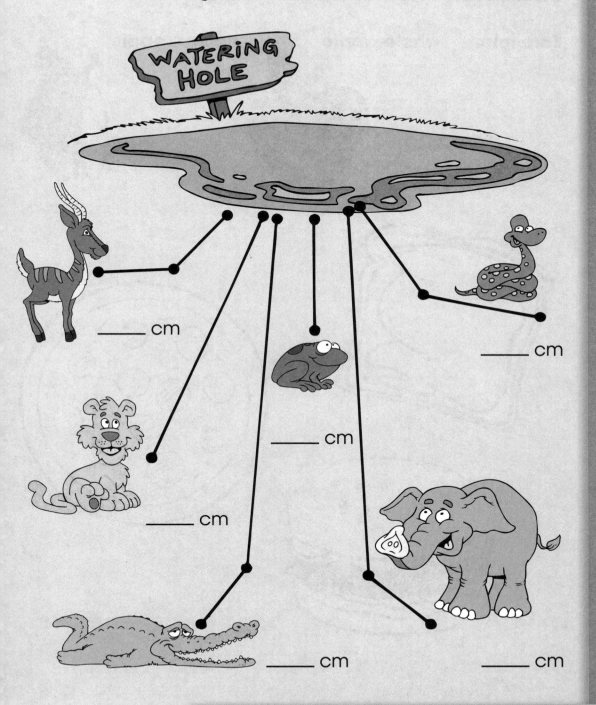

_____ cm

_____ cm

_____ cm

_____ cm

_____ cm

_____ cm

_____ cm

MATH

One Step Further
In centimeters, measure the distance from your bed to your dresser.

Whole and Half

A **fraction** is a number that names part of a whole, such as $\frac{1}{2}$.

Directions: Color half of each thing.

Example: whole apple   half an apple

One Step Further
Divide a piece of toast into two equal halves.
Eat one half. How much is left?

One Third

Directions: Complete the fraction statements.

Example:

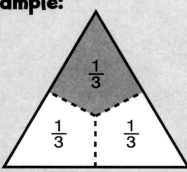

 part is blue.

The parts are the same size.

 of the inside is blue.

___ part is blue.

___ parts are the same size.

___ of the inside is blue.

___ part is blue.

___ parts are the same size.

___ of the inside is blue.

___ part is blue.

___ parts are the same size.

___ of the inside is blue.

___ part is blue.

___ parts are the same size.

___ of the inside is blue.

MATH

One Step Further

Draw a rectangle and draw a picture inside it. Divide the rectangle into three parts.

One Fourth

Directions: Complete the fraction statements.

Example:

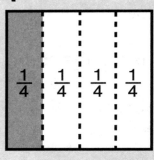 part is blue.

The 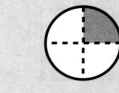 parts are the same size.

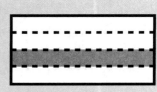 of the inside is blue.

 _____ part is blue.

 _____ parts are the same size.

_____ of the inside is blue.

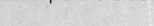

_____ part is blue.

_____ parts are the same size.

_____ of the inside is blue.

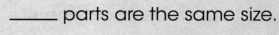

_____ part is blue.

_____ parts are the same size.

_____ of the inside is blue.

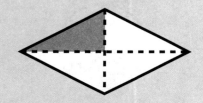

_____ part is blue.

_____ parts are the same size.

_____ of the inside is blue.

One Step Further
Fold a piece of construction paper into fourths. Draw a picture on each part.

Half, Third, Fourth

Directions: Color the shapes to show each fraction. Some shapes will not be used.

Example:

shaded part   **1**
equal parts   **2**

$\frac{1}{2}$ (one-half)

shaded part   **1**
equal parts   **3**

$\frac{1}{3}$ (one-third)

shaded part   **1**
equal parts   **4**

$\frac{1}{4}$ (one-fourth)

Color $\frac{1}{3}$ **red** 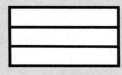

Color $\frac{1}{4}$ **blue** 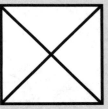

Color $\frac{1}{2}$ **orange** 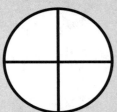

One Step Further

Find three bananas. Divide one in half, one in thirds, and one in fourths.

Fraction Food

Directions: Count the equal parts. Circle the fraction that names one of the parts.

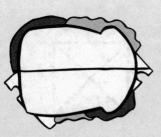

$\frac{1}{2}$ $\frac{1}{3}$ $\frac{1}{4}$

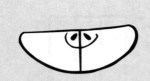

$\frac{1}{2}$ $\frac{1}{3}$ $\frac{1}{4}$

$\frac{1}{2}$ $\frac{1}{3}$ $\frac{1}{4}$

$\frac{1}{2}$ $\frac{1}{3}$ $\frac{1}{4}$

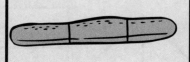

$\frac{1}{2}$ $\frac{1}{3}$ $\frac{1}{4}$

$\frac{1}{2}$ $\frac{1}{3}$ $\frac{1}{4}$

$\frac{1}{2}$ $\frac{1}{3}$ $\frac{1}{4}$

$\frac{1}{2}$ $\frac{1}{3}$ $\frac{1}{4}$

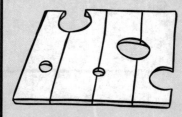

$\frac{1}{2}$ $\frac{1}{3}$ $\frac{1}{4}$

One Step Further

What's for dinner tonight?
Divide your food into three equal piles.

Second Grade Essentials

Games and Activities

GAMES

Fun Foods

Directions: Look at the picture clues. Then, complete the puzzle using the words from the word box.

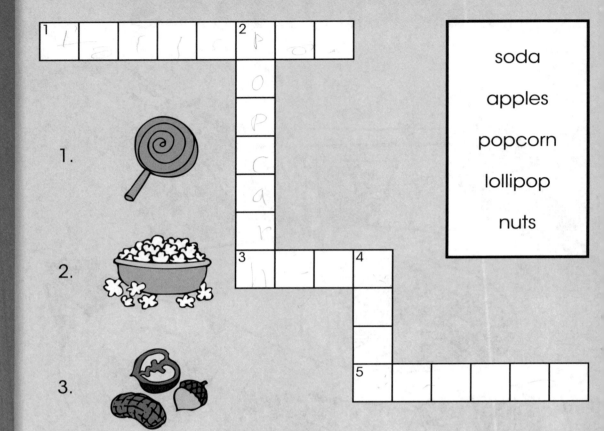

1. (across) l e l l i p o p

Word box:

- soda
- apples
- popcorn
- lollipop
- nuts

1.
2.
3.
4.
5.

One Step Further

Plan, shop for, and prepare a healthy snack. Serve it to friends at a movie party.

At the Market

Directions: Circle the words in the puzzle. The words go across and down. Can you find an extra word?

```
b g c o s a l t e l m p o l
r p e a c h e s a p w f j y
e h l h s h t o c s e i r e
a m e a t l r u e q r s p o
d i r i b a p p l e s h d c
o l y l g g x d a p o l p l
s k i p o p s i c l e a s w
t z n c h e e s e r i t k v
```

cheese	soup
bread	peaches
meat	fish
milk	salt
celery	apples

The extra word I found is _____.

One Step Further

Look at a grocery ad. Find a price for each item on the list. What would be the total price?

GAMES

Second Grade Essentials

Awesome Animals

Directions: Circle the words in the puzzle. The words go across and down.

```
q h w b j t u r t l e
m o n k e y k g p c l
i r s p g i r a f f e
g s l d o f w o n l p
z e b r a f h e r h h
d a l l i g a t o r a
m f r u d o l p h i n
s n a k e r e v a k t
```

elephant	horse
giraffe	whale
alligator	snake
dolphin	zebra
turtle	monkey

One Step Further

Use toys to make a zoo. Make a sign for each animal enclosure and a map for guests.

GAMES

Amphibians and Reptiles

Directions: Read the clues and use the words in the word box to complete the puzzle.

amphibian

reptile

turtle

crocodile

frog

Across

2. A ____ is a reptile that has a shell and pulls its head, legs, and tail into the shell for protection.
3. An ____ is a cold-blooded animal that has scaleless skin and lives part of its life in water.
5. A ____ is a reptile that has a long snout.

Down

1. A ____ is a cold-blooded animal that has dry, scaly skin.
4. A ____ is an amphibian that has four legs and no tail.

One Step Further

If a sea turtle lays 100 eggs three times each year, how many eggs would it lay in three years?

Time for a Scrub!

Directions: Help the robin find the birdbath.

One Step Further

Find a list of birds common to your area. How
many birds from the list have you seen?

GAMES

For the Birds

Directions: Fit the bird words from the cloud into the puzzle.

1. j **a** y
2. o **w** l
3. e a **g** l e
4. r o b i n
5. p a r r o **t** s
6. **o** s t r i c h
7. p i g **e** o n s
8. **b** u z z a r d

buzzard   robin
jay   parrots
pigeons   eagle
ostrich   owl

One Step Further

Roll a stale bagel in peanut butter and bird-seed. Tie it to a branch outside for the birds.

Second Grade Essentials

Here Kitty Kitty!

Directions: See how many times you find the word **kitty** in the puzzle. Color the boxes to show the word. Be sure to look down and across.

k	i	y	k	i	t	t	y	k
i	t	k	i	t	t	y	t	t
k	i	t	t	y	y	i	k	t
i	t	y	t	k	i	t	t	y
y	t	k	y	k	i	t	t	y

GAMES

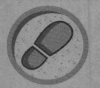

One Step Further
The Spanish word for **cat** is **el gato**. Learn how to say **cat** in another language.

Little Ones

Directions: Look at the picture clues. Then, complete the puzzle using the words from the word box.

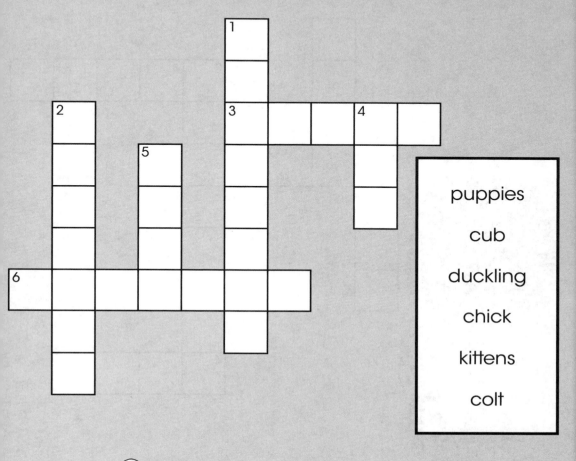

puppies

cub

duckling

chick

kittens

colt

GAMES

1.    2.    3.

4.   5.    6.

One Step Further
A baby deer is a fawn. A baby goose is a gosling. Find three more baby animal names.

Living Things

Directions: Read the clues and use the words in the tree to complete the puzzle.

girl
flower
tree
eagle
fish
elephant

Across
2. I can fly.
3. I am a plant. I have petals and smell pretty.
4. I have a trunk, leaves, and branches.

Down
1. I am a person.
2. I am a large gray animal with a long trunk and big, floppy ears.
3. I live in the water and can swim.

One Step Further
Go outside and turn in a circle. How many living things do you see?

Nonliving Things

Directions: Read the clues and use the words in the word box to complete the puzzle.

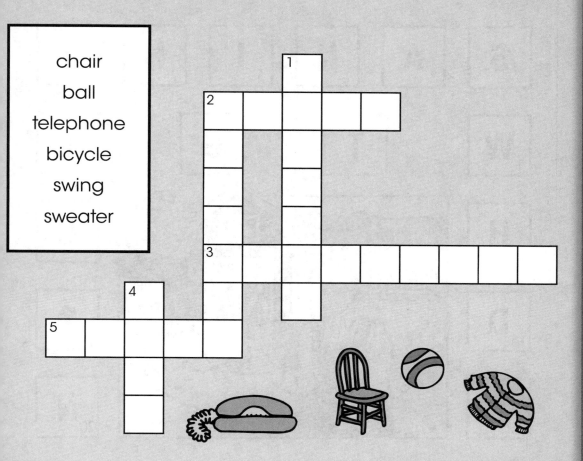

| chair |
| ball |
| telephone |
| bicycle |
| swing |
| sweater |

Across

2. A ____ is something you play on.
3. A ____ is something you call people on to talk to them.
5. A ____ is something that has four legs and you sit on it.

Down

1. A ____ is something you ride on that has two wheels.
2. A ____ is something you wear to keep you warm.
4. A ____ is something you can throw and catch.

One Step Further

Call out a letter. How many things can you and a friend name that begin with the letter?

Second Grade Essentials

A Final Question

Directions: Match the scrambled letters to find out what the farmer wants to ask.

S 5	A 3	N 7	I 6	H 9	T 8
W 1		T 4	G 13		E 10
H 2					B 11
D 16					? 21
E 15					N 20
B 17	R 14	R 19	R 18		I 12

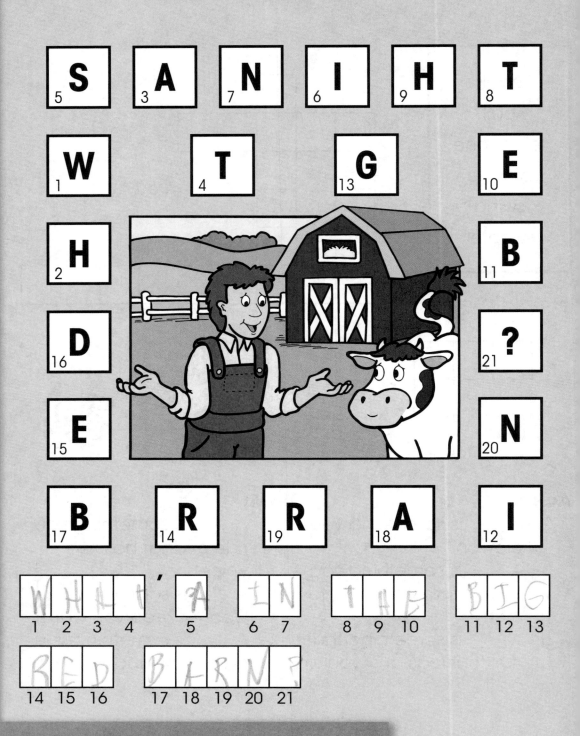

W	H	A	T	'	A		I	N		T	H	E		B	I	G
1	2	3	4		5		6	7		8	9	10		11	12	13

R	E	D		B	A	R	N	?
14	15	16		17	18	19	20	21

One Step Further

How would you spend your day on a farm?
Write a schedule for each hour of the day.

Barnyard Adventure

Directions: Help the children get to the barn.

GAMES

One Step Further
What would be your favorite chore to do on a farm? Why?

Bath Time

Directions: Help the boy get to the bathtub.

One Step Further
Get a bucket of soapy water and a sponge.
Use them to wash your bike, toys, or dog!

In the Bathroom

Directions: Circle the words in the puzzle. The words go across, down, and diagonally.

```
t o o t h b r u s h p b m
s h a m p o o a i q t a i
a o x l i g h t n r b t r
s y a w z r o s k t c h r
h v u p s n u t d o x t o
o b t e r m k g e w f u r
w a s h c l o t h e g b g
e f a u c e t o n l i k h
r c d f l q p j i m h l j
```

toothbrush	towel
mirror	faucet
soap	rug
sink	shampoo
bathtub	shower
washcloth	light

One Step Further
Dentists recommend brushing your teeth for two minutes. Time yourself as you brush.

GAMES

Pet Time

Directions: Look in the bone for the things you might need for a new pet. Write the words in the puzzle.

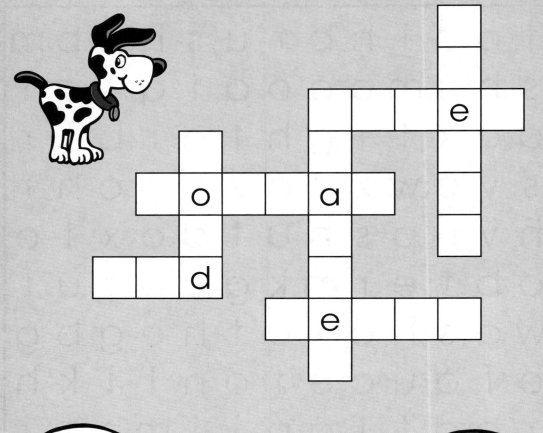

leash   food   collar   treats
bones   bed   blanket

One Step Further
How much does a 10 pound bag of dog food cost? Research to find out.

Where's the Bone?

Directions: Help the dog find the bone.

One Step Further
Make bone-shaped cards from paper. Invent your own card game to play.

Fish

Directions: Read the clues and use the words in the word box to complete the puzzle.

colors

lakes

mouths

ocean

fins

gills

Across
1. Saltwater fish live in the ____.
3. Fish open and close their ____ as they swim to get air from the water.
4. The water comes out of their ____.
6. Fish have tails and ____.

Down
2. Fish are many different sizes, shapes, and ____.
5. Freshwater fish live in ponds, rivers, or ____.

One Step Further
Cut fish shapes from colored paper. Write a math fact on each one.

Spouting About

Directions: To find the mystery letter, color the spaces with the following letters yellow.

e m c q y r o j a

e	b	s	d
q	k	t	f
c	a	m	i
o	g	y	n
r	h	j	p

Directions: Circle the mystery letter.

d   h   m

One Step Further

Which whales fly? Pilot whales! Think of more whale jokes to tell your friends.

GAMES

Fruity Fun

Directions: Read the word for each picture. Write the words in the puzzle.

Across

2. plum

3. apple

5.  grapes

Down

1. orange

2. pear

4. peach

One Step Further

Mix up a smoothie. Use at least two different fruits. Write your recipe.

Plants We Eat

Directions: Read the clues and use the words in the word box to complete the puzzle.

carrot

rhubarb

lettuce

corn

peach

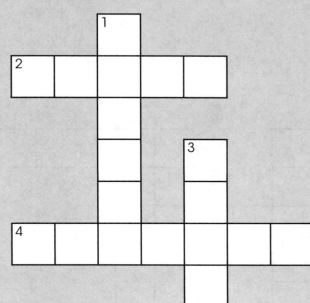

GAMES

Across
2. When we eat a ____, we are eating the fruit of a plant.
4. When we eat ____, we are eating the leaves of a plant.
5. When we eat ____, we are eating the seeds of a plant.

Down
1. When we eat a ____, we are eating the root of a plant.
3. When we eat ____, we are eating the stem of a plant.

One Step Further
Plant a seed and keep it moist. How many days does it take to sprout?

Second Grade Essentials

Land and Water

Directions: Read the clues and use the words in the word box to complete the puzzle.

mountain

valley

plain

ocean

lake

river

Across

2. This is a body of fresh water surrounded by land.
4. This is a very high hill.
6. This is low land between mountains or hills.

Down

1. This is a very flat stretch of land.
3. This is a flowing stream of water.
5. This is a large body of salt water.

One Step Further

Use clay and other materials to sculpt land-forms and bodies of water on a cookie tray.

Out in Space

Directions: On the lines, write the name of the object shown in the picture.

1. ___ ___ u ___ ___

2. ___ ___ o ___ ___

3. ___ ___ ___ ___ ___ ___ n ___

4. ___ ___ ___ ___ ___ ___ ___

5. ___ t ___ ___

6. ___ ___ ___ ___ ___ h

7. ___ ___ m ___ ___

8. ___ ___ ___ ___ ___

star	Earth	rocket	Pluto
moon	comet	Saturn	Venus

One Step Further
Choose one planet in our solar system. Learn three facts about it.

Forest Life

Directions: Read the clues and use the words in the word box to complete the puzzle.

sunlight

insects

squirrels

forest

trees

deer

Across

3. ____ climb trees and eat acorns.
5. Many ____ crawl along the forest floor.
6. Many ____ grow in the forest.

Down

1. A little bit of ____ shines through the trees.
2. It is cool and dark in the ____.
4. A ____ nibbles on the sweet green plants.

One Step Further

Take pictures during a walk through the woods. Make a forest photo collage.

Busy Beaver

Directions: Help the beaver find the water.

One Step Further

What does "busy as a beaver" mean? What other animal sayings can you think of?

Squaring Up

Directions: Use a word from the box to complete each sentence. Then, write each word in the puzzle.

1				2

|3| | | | |

kite

caps

snake

clock

Across

1. The ___ ___ ___ ___ ___ said it was two o'clock.

3. The ___ ___ ___ ___ ___ slithered in the grass.

Down

1. Tommy has three baseball ___ ___ ___ ___.

2. I flew my ___ ___ ___ ___ at the beach.

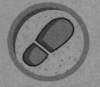

One Step Further

Research different kinds of kites on the Internet. Which is your favorite?

In the Desk

Directions: Circle the words in the puzzle. The words go across and down.

```
j o p e n c i l m n g t c l
n f a n b f c x r x e a r p
l o p v e r a s e r m p a a
k p e n b v c x w k o e y i
m k r s t a p l e r v r o n
f r e l m n i j n b t n n t
m n o t e b o o k m h n s s
v r d c j o l p l o m n b f
```

pencil   pen
paper   eraser
stapler   paints
crayons   tape
notebook

GAMES

One Step Further
Should students share supplies or use their own? Write to explain your opinion.

School Days

Directions: Circle the words in the puzzle. The words go across, down, and diagonally.

```
p t k l r t e a c h e r t
u a e r a s e r r u t s s
g f p m q n o p a d e s c
h j p e n c i l y r s v i
g e i y r h a w o p t h s
v l x z z a d x n q g i s
w d u c y l e b s f k j o
b a d e s k c p a i n t r
c o m p u t e r l m o n s
```

paper   eraser   glue

pencil   chalk   scissors

test   crayons   teacher

desk   paint   computer

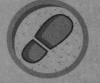

One Step Further

Design an activity for your class. What supplies would you need? Share with your teacher.

Second Grade Essentials

Keyboard Crazy

Directions: To find the mystery letter, color the spaces with the following letters **green**.

N C M E R H F P T B G S A

Directions: Circle the mystery letter.

B K N

One Step Further

Invent a computer password. Choose letters and numbers that are meaningful to you.

GAMES

Second Grade Essentials

Career Time

Directions: Use the pictures and words to help you fill in the puzzle.

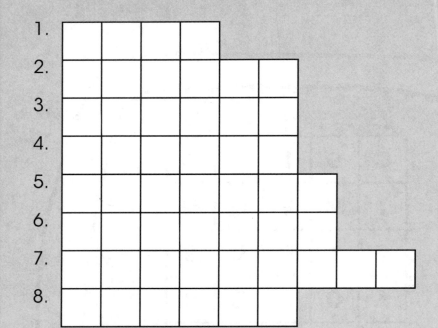

1.
2.
3.
4.
5.
6.
7.
8.

doctor

teacher

artist

plumber

lawyer

singer

chef

carpenter

1.

2.

3.

4.

5.

6.

7.

8.

One Step Further

What do you want to be when you grow up?
Make a sign for your future workplace.

Getting Dressed

Directions: Look at the picture clues. Then, complete the puzzle using the words from the word box.

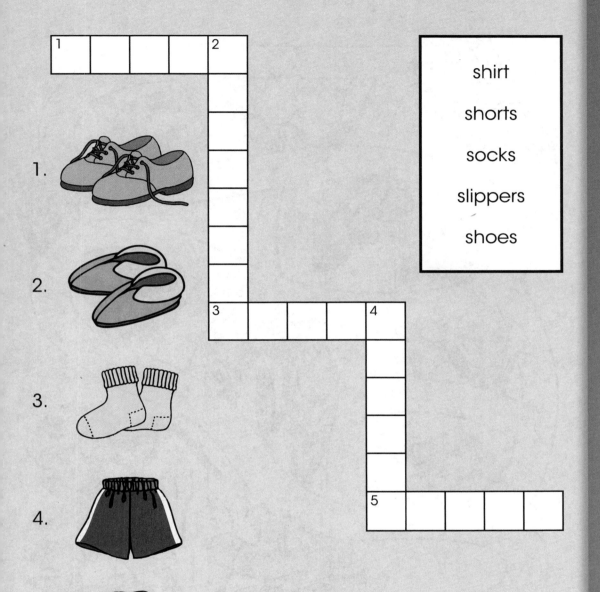

Word box:
shirt
shorts
socks
slippers
shoes

1.
2.
3.
4.
5.

One Step Further
Clean out your closet and drawers. Give outgrown clothes to a younger child or to charity.

Fly Away Home

Directions: Help the butterfly find the butterfly house.

One Step Further
Draw the life stages of a butterfly: egg, caterpillar, chrysalis, adult.

At the Pond

Directions: Read the clues and use the words in the word box to complete the puzzle.

cattails

lily pad

turtle

fish

willow

pond

Across

4. A bullfrog sits on a ____ and croaks a loud song.
5. A family of ducks waddle into the ____ for a swim.
6. A raccoon tries to catch a ____ as it swims by.

Down

1. A ____ sits on a rock in the morning sun.
2. The weeping ____ gives shade to the animals.
3. Birds fly over the many ____ sticking out of the water.

GAMES

One Step Further

Take a magnifying glass to a pond or stream near you. What do you see?

Parts of a Plant

Directions: Read the clues and use the words in the word box to complete the puzzle.

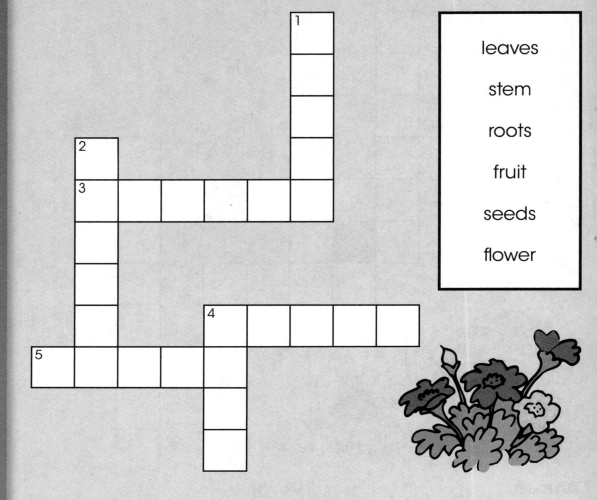

Word box:
leaves

stem

roots

fruit

seeds

flower

Across

3. They make food for the plant.
4. New plants grow from these.
5. This covers and protects the seeds.

Down

1. These take in water and minerals from the soil.
2. This is the part where the seeds are formed.
4. It carries the water and minerals to the leaves.

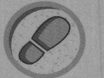

One Step Further

Find a plant and observe it closely. Make a detailed drawing. Label each part of the plant.

In My Garden

Directions: Circle the words in the puzzle. The words go across and down.

j	p	o	g	q	p	e	a	s	c
b	e	r	r	i	e	s	d	b	a
e	a	n	a	t	a	f	n	k	r
c	c	o	p	l	v	s	c	h	r
o	h	f	e	t	o	m	a	t	o
r	e	w	s	r	u	p	r	i	t
n	s	y	c	m	b	e	a	n	s

tomato   peaches   berries

corn   grapes   peas

beans

carrots

One Step Further

Draw a garden plot with 12 rows. What vegetables would you plant in each row?

Second Grade Essentials

What's the Mystery?

Directions: Use the pictures to help you fill in the puzzle. Then, use the words you wrote in the sentences below.

1			2
3			

leak

lock

mail

meal

Across

1. He ate the ___ ___ ___ ___.

3. The ___ ___ ___ ___ is on the door.

Down

1. Please open the ___ ___ ___ ___.

2. Does that pipe ___ ___ ___ ___?

One Step Further

Give a friend three clues to a number. Can your friend guess the number?

GAMES

It's a Square

Directions: Use the words in the word box to finish each sentence. Then, use the same words in the puzzle.

Across

1. He is at _____.

3. I will ride my _____.

home
easy
help
pony

Down

1. Mother will _____ us.

2. It is an _____ job.

GAMES

One Step Further
What would be good about having a pony?
What would be difficult? Make two lists.

Super Stars

Directions: Write the events from the Olympics in the spaces. Find the secret words in the center boxes when you finish.

1. water polo
2.
3. s
4. s
5. t
6. k
7.
8. j
9. g
10. c
11. r
12. c
13. ice skating

gymnastics	soccer	track	pole vault
swimming	skiing	javelin	
shot put	discus throw	diving	
marathon	ice skating	water polo	

One Step Further

With an adult, watch an Internet video that shows a sport you would like to try.

Time for Music

Directions: Write the music words in the boxes.

1.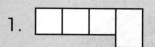

2.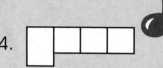

3.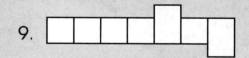

4.

5.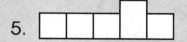

6.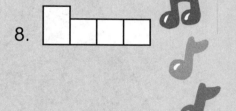

7.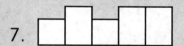

8.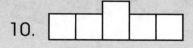

9.

10.

| song | classical | scale | staff | country |
| notes | tune | rock | jazz | rhythm |

One Step Further
Ask 10 people to tell their favorite type of music. Make a graph to show the results.

Second Grade Essentials

Answer Key

ANSWER KEY

6

All About Me!

Directions: Fill in the blanks to tell all about you!

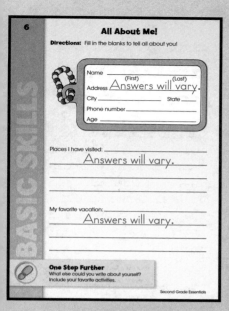

Name _____
(First)   (Last)
Address _Answers will vary._
City _____ State ____
Phone number _____
Age _____

Places I have visited:
Answers will vary.
_____
_____
_____

My favorite vacation:
Answers will vary.
_____
_____
_____

One Step Further
What else could you write about yourself?
Include your favorite activities.

Second Grade Essentials

7

Parts of a Book

A book has many parts. The **title** is the name of the book. The **author** is the person who wrote the words. The **illustrator** is the person who drew the pictures. The **table of contents** is located at the beginning to list what is in the book. The **glossary** is a little dictionary in the back to help you with unfamiliar words. Books are often divided into smaller sections of information called **chapters**.

Directions: Look at one of your books. Write the parts you see below.

The title of my book is _Answers will vary._

The author is _____

The illustrator is _____

My book has a table of contents.   Yes or No

My book has a glossary.   Yes or No

My book is divided into chapters.   Yes or No

One Step Further
What else can you tell about your book?
What category would it fit into at the library?

Second Grade Essentials

8

ABC Order

Directions: Put the words in ABC order on the bags.

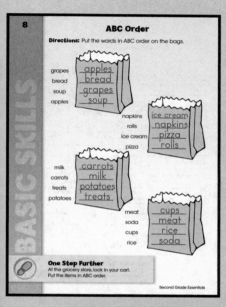

grapes
bread
soup
apples

apples
bread
grapes
soup

napkins
rolls
ice cream
pizza

ice cream
napkins
pizza
rolls

milk
carrots
treats
potatoes

carrots
milk
potatoes
treats

meat
soda
cups
rice

cups
meat
rice
soda

One Step Further
At the grocery store, look in your cart.
Put the items in ABC order.

Second Grade Essentials

9

ABC Order

Directions: Write these words in order. If two words start with the same letter, look at the second letter in each word.

Example: lamb   **Lamb** is first because **a** comes before **i**
light   in the alphabet.

tree   branch
branch   leaf
leaf   tree

dish   bone
dog   dish
bone   dog

rain   cloud
umbrella   rain
cloud   umbrella

One Step Further
Choose three objects from your bookbag.
Put them in ABC order.

Second Grade Essentials

10

ABC Order

If the first letters of two words are the same, look at the second letters in both words. If the second letters are the same, look at the third letters.

Directions: Write 1, 2, 3, or 4 on the lines in each row to put the words in ABC order. The first one has been done for you.

1. **1** candy **2** carrot **4** duck **3** dance

2. **2** cold **4** hot **1** carry **3** hit

3. **2** flash **1** fan **3** fun **4** garden

4. **2** seat **4** sun **1** saw **3** sit

5. **3** row **1** ring **2** rock **4** run

6. **2** truck **3** turn **4** twin **1** talk

One Step Further
Write four words. Ask a friend to put them in ABC order.

Second Grade Essentials

11

ABC Order

Kwan likes to make rhymes. Help Kwan think of rhyming words.

Directions: Write three words in ABC order that rhyme with each word Kwan wrote.

cap   bet   bill
Answers will vary.
_____
_____

dog   man   hat
_____
_____
_____

Directions: Write a short poem using some of the rhyming words you wrote.
Answers will vary.
_____
_____
_____

One Step Further
Choose two rhyming words from this page.
Can you find both objects in your home?

Second Grade Essentials

Second Grade Essentials

12

Syllables

Words are made up of parts called **syllables**. Each syllable has a vowel sound. One way to count syllables is to clap as you say the word.

Example:
cat	one clap	one syllable
table	two claps	two syllables
butterfly	three claps	three syllables

Directions: "Clap out" the words below. Write how many syllables each word has.

movie	two	dog	one
piano	three	basket	two
tree	one	swimmer	two
bicycle	three	rainbow	two
sun	one	paper	two
cabinet	three	picture	two

One Step Further
Clap as you say your first name out loud.
How many syllables does your name have?

Second Grade Essentials

13

Syllables

Dividing a word into syllables can help you read a new word. You also might divide syllables when you are writing if you run out of space on a line.

Many words contain two consonants that are next to each other. A word can usually be divided between the consonants.

Directions: Divide each word into two syllables. The first one has been done for you.

kitten	**kit ten**
lumber	lum ber
batter	bat ter
winter	win ter
funny	fun ny
harder	har der
dirty	dir ty
sister	sis ter
little	lit tle

One Step Further
What is the name of your school?
How many syllables does it have?

Second Grade Essentials

14

Syllables

One way to help you read a word you don't know is to divide it into parts called **syllables**. Every syllable has a vowel sound.

Directions: Say the words. Write the number of syllables.

straw • ber • ry

bird	one	rabbit	two
apple	two	elephant	three
balloon	two	family	three
basketball	three	fence	one
breakfast	two	ladder	two
block	one	open	two
candy	two	puddle	two
popcorn	two	Saturday	three

One Step Further
Find a book. Choose a sentence and divide each word into syllables.

Second Grade Essentials

15

Syllables

When a double consonant is used in the middle of a word, the word can usually be divided between the consonants.

Directions: Look at the words in the word box. Divide each word into two syllables. Leave space between each syllable. One is done for you.

butter	pillow	chatter	kitten	mitten	happy
dinner	puppy	letter	ladder	yellow	summer

but ter	chat ter	mit ten
din ner	let ter	yel low
pil low	kit ten	hap py
pup py	lad der	sum mer

Many words are divided between two consonants that are not alike.

Directions: Look at the words in the word box. Divide each word into two syllables. One is done for you.

window	barber	winter	number	picture	candle
mister	doctor	sister	pencil	carpet	under

win dow	win ter	pic ture
mis ter	sis ter	car pet
bar ber	num ber	can dle
doc tor	pen cil	un der

One Step Further
Walk around your neighborhood.
Divide all the objects you see into syllables.

Second Grade Essentials

16

Syllables

Directions: Write 1 or 2 on the line to tell how many syllables are in each word. If the word has two syllables, draw a line between the syllables.

Example: sup|per

dog	1	timber	2
bedroom	2	cat	1
slipper	2	street	1
tree	1	chalk	1
batter	2	blanket	2
chair	1	marker	2
fish	1	brush	1

One Step Further
Can you name a word that has three syllables? Four syllables?

Second Grade Essentials

17

Learning Dictionary Skills

A **dictionary** is a book that gives the meaning of words. It also tells how words sound. Words in a dictionary are in ABC order. That makes them easier to find. A picture dictionary lists a word, a picture of the word, and its meaning.

Directions: Look at this page from a picture dictionary. Then, answer the questions.

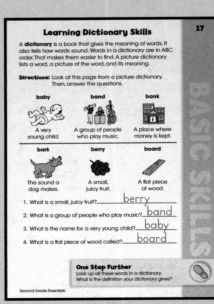

baby	**band**	**bank**
A very young child.	A group of people who play music.	A place where money is kept.

bark	**berry**	**board**
The sound a dog makes.	A small, juicy fruit.	A flat piece of wood.

1. What is a small, juicy fruit? berry
2. What is a group of people who play music? band
3. What is the name for a very young child? baby
4. What is a flat piece of wood called? board

One Step Further
Look up all these words in a dictionary.
What is the definition your dictionary gives?

Second Grade Essentials

ANSWER KEY

18

Learning Dictionary Skills

Directions: Look at this page from a picture dictionary. Then, answer the questions.

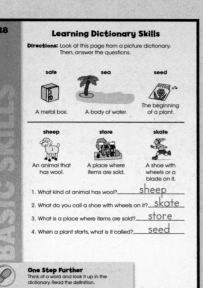

safe — A metal box.
sea — A body of water.
seed — The beginning of a plant.

sheep — An animal that has wool.
store — A place where items are sold.
skate — A shoe with wheels or a blade on it.

1. What kind of animal has wool? __sheep__
2. What do you call a shoe with wheels on it? __skate__
3. What is a place where items are sold? __store__
4. When a plant starts, what is it called? __seed__

One Step Further
Think of a word and look it up in the dictionary. Read the definition.

Second Grade Essentials

19

Learning Dictionary Skills

Directions: Look at this page from a picture dictionary. Then, answer the questions.

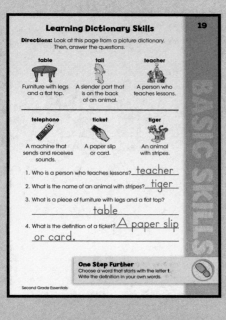

table — Furniture with legs and a flat top.
tail — A slender part that is on the back of an animal.
teacher — A person who teaches lessons.

telephone — A machine that sends and receives sounds.
ticket — A paper slip or card.
tiger — An animal with stripes.

1. Who is a person who teaches lessons? __teacher__
2. What is the name of an animal with stripes? __tiger__
3. What is a piece of furniture with legs and a flat top? __table__
4. What is the definition of a ticket? __A paper slip or card.__

One Step Further
Choose a word that starts with the letter **t**. Write the definition in your own words.

Second Grade Essentials

20

Stuffed Animals

Kate and Oralia like to collect and trade stuffed animals.

Directions: Draw two stuffed animals that are alike and two that are different.

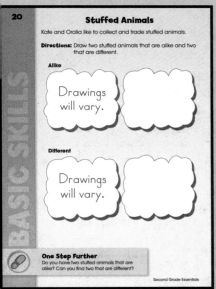

Alike
Drawings will vary.

Different
Drawings will vary.

One Step Further
Do you have two stuffed animals that are alike? Can you find two that are different?

Second Grade Essentials

21

Shell Homes

Directions: Read about shells. Then, answer the questions.

Shells are the homes of some animals. Snails live in shells on the land. Clams live in shells in the water. Clam shells open. Snail shells stay closed. Both shells keep the animals safe.

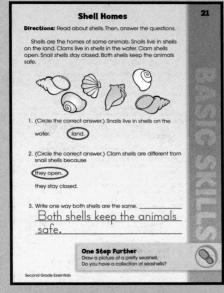

1. (Circle the correct answer.) Snails live in shells on the water. (land.)

2. (Circle the correct answer.) Clam shells are different from snail shells because (they open.) they stay closed.

3. Write one way both shells are the same. __Both shells keep the animals safe.__

One Step Further
Draw a picture of a pretty seashell. Do you have a collection of seashells?

Second Grade Essentials

22

Venn Diagram

A **Venn diagram** is a diagram that shows how two things are the same and different.

Directions: Choose two outdoor sports. Then, follow the instructions to complete the Venn diagram.

1. Write the first sport name under the first circle. Write some words that describe the sport. Write them in the first circle.

2. Write the second sport name under the second circle. Write some words that describe the sport. Write them in the circle.

3. Where the two circles overlap, write some words that describe both sports.

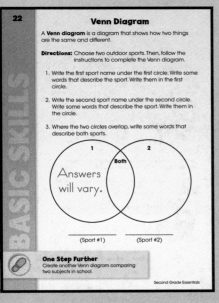

1   **Both**   2

Answers will vary.

(Sport #1)   (Sport #2)

One Step Further
Create another Venn diagram comparing two subjects in school.

Second Grade Essentials

23

Dina and Dina

Directions: Read the story. Then, complete the Venn diagram, telling how Dina, the duck, is the same or different than Dina, the girl.

One day in the library, Dina found a story about a duck named Dina!

My name is Dina. I am a duck, and I like to swim. When I am not swimming, I walk on land or fly. I have two feet and two eyes. My feathers keep me warm. Ducks can be different colors. I am gray, brown, and black. I really like being a duck. It is fun.

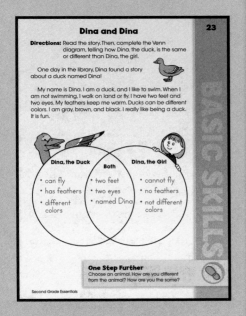

Dina, the Duck
• can fly
• has feathers
• different colors

Both
• two feet
• two eyes
• named Dina

Dina, the Girl
• cannot fly
• no feathers
• not different colors

One Step Further
Choose an animal. How are you different from the animal? How are you the same?

Second Grade Essentials

Second Grade Essentials

24

Cats and Tigers

Directions: Read about cats and tigers. Then, complete the Venn diagram, telling how they are the same and different.

Tigers are a kind of cat. Pet cats and tigers both have fur. Pet cats are small and tame. Tigers are large and wild.

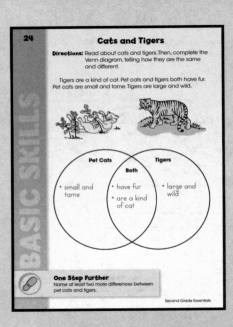

Pet Cats | **Both** | **Tigers**
- small and tame
- have fur
- are a kind of cat
- large and wild

One Step Further
Name at least two more differences between pet cats and tigers.

Second Grade Essentials

25

Bluebirds and Parrots

Directions: Read about parrots and bluebirds. Then, complete the Venn diagram, telling how they are the same and different.

Bluebirds and parrots are both birds. Bluebirds and parrots can fly. They both have beaks. Parrots can live inside a cage. Bluebirds must live outdoors.

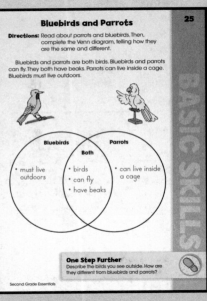

Bluebirds | **Both** | **Parrots**
- must live outdoors
- birds
- can fly
- have beaks
- can live inside a cage

One Step Further
Describe the birds you see outside. How are they different from bluebirds and parrots?

Second Grade Essentials

26

Heavy Hitters

Fiction is a make-believe story. **Nonfiction** is a true story.

Directions: Read the stories about two famous baseball players. Then, write **fiction** or **nonfiction** in the baseball bats.

Even if you are not a baseball fan, you might know who Jackie Robinson was. African American players were not allowed to play in the major leagues. Then, in 1947, Jackie joined the Brooklyn Dodgers. He was the first African American player in the major leagues. People said hateful things to him. But Jackie was strong and did not fight back. He made history and became one of the best major league players ever!

nonfiction

The Mighty Casey played baseball for the Mudville Nine and was the greatest of all baseball players. He could hit the cover off the ball with the power of a hurricane. But, when the Mudville Nine was losing 4-2 in the championship game, Mighty Casey struck out with the bases loaded. There was no joy in Mudville that day, because the Mudville Nine had lost the game.

fiction

One Step Further
Do you know any other famous baseball players? Tell a story about baseball.

Second Grade Essentials

27

Tornado Tips

Directions: Read about tornadoes. Then, follow the instructions.

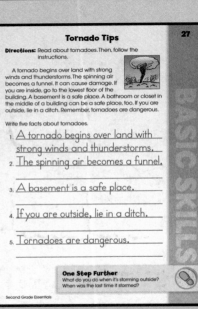

A tornado begins over land with strong winds and thunderstorms. The spinning air becomes a funnel. It can cause damage. If you are inside, go to the lowest floor of the building. A basement is a safe place. A bathroom or closet in the middle of a building can be a safe place, too. If you are outside, lie in a ditch. Remember, tornadoes are dangerous.

Write five facts about tornadoes.

1. A tornado begins over land with strong winds and thunderstorms.
2. The spinning air becomes a funnel.
3. A basement is a safe place.
4. If you are outside, lie in a ditch.
5. Tornadoes are dangerous.

One Step Further
What do you do when it's storming outside? When was the last time it stormed?

Second Grade Essentials

28

Hercules

The **setting** is where a story takes place. The **characters** are the people in a story or play.

Directions: Read about Hercules. Then, answer the questions.

Hercules was born in the warm Atlantic Ocean. He was a very small and weak baby. He wanted to be the strongest hurricane in the world. But he had one problem. He couldn't blow 75-mile-per-hour winds. Hercules blew and blew in the ocean, until one day, his sister, Hola, told him it would be more fun to be a breeze than a hurricane. Hercules agreed. It was a breeze to be a breeze!

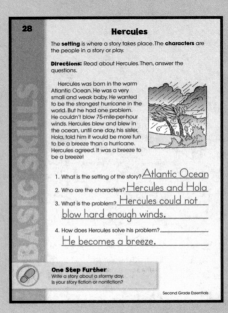

1. What is the setting of the story? Atlantic Ocean
2. Who are the characters? Hercules and Hola
3. What is the problem? Hercules could not blow hard enough winds.
4. How does Hercules solve his problem? He becomes a breeze.

One Step Further
Write a story about a stormy day. Is your story fiction or nonfiction?

Second Grade Essentials

29

The Fourth of July

Directions: Read each story. Then, write whether it is fiction or nonfiction.

One sunny day in July, a dog named Stan ran away from home. He went up one street and down the other looking for fun, but all the yards were empty. Where was everybody? Stan kept walking until he heard the sound of band music and happy people. Stan walked faster until he got to Central Street. There he saw men, women, children, and dogs getting ready to walk in a parade. It was the Fourth of July!

Fiction or nonfiction? fiction

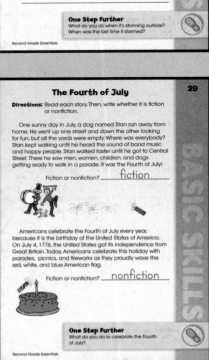

Americans celebrate the Fourth of July every year, because it is the birthday of the United States of America. On July 4, 1776, the United States got its independence from Great Britain. Today, Americans celebrate this holiday with parades, picnics, and fireworks as they proudly wave the red, white, and blue American flag.

Fiction or nonfiction? nonfiction

One Step Further
What do you do to celebrate the Fourth of July?

Second Grade Essentials

Which Is It?

30

Directions: Read about fiction and nonfiction books. Then, follow the instructions.

There are many kinds of books. Some books have make-believe stories about princesses and dragons. Some books contain poetry and rhymes, like Mother Goose. These are fiction.

Some books contain facts about space and plants. And still other books have stories about famous people in history, like Abraham Lincoln. These are nonfiction.

Write **F** for fiction and **NF** for nonfiction.

F __ 1. nursery rhyme
F __ 2. fairy tale
NF __ 3. true-life story of a famous athlete
F __ 4. Aesop's fables
NF __ 5. dictionary entry about foxes
NF __ 6. weather report
F __ 7. story about a talking tree
NF __ 8. story about how a tadpole becomes a frog

One Step Further
What books do you most like to read, fiction or nonfiction? Why?

Second Grade Essentials

Games!

31

A **fact** is something that can be proven. An **opinion** is a feeling or belief about something and cannot be proven.

Directions: Read these sentences about different games. Then, write **F** next to each fact and **O** next to each opinion.

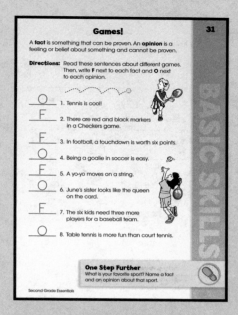

O __ 1. Tennis is cool!
F __ 2. There are red and black markers in a Checkers game.
F __ 3. In football, a touchdown is worth six points.
O __ 4. Being a goalie in soccer is easy.
F __ 5. A yo-yo moves on a string.
O __ 6. June's sister looks like the queen on the card.
F __ 7. The six kids need three more players for a baseball team.
O __ 8. Table tennis is more fun than court tennis.

One Step Further
What is your favorite sport? Name a fact and an opinion about that sport.

Second Grade Essentials

Recycling

32

Directions: Read about recycling. Then, follow the instructions.

What do you throw away every day? What could you do with these things? You could change an old greeting card into a new card. You could make a puppet with an old paper bag. Old buttons make great refrigerator magnets. You can plant seeds in plastic cups. Cardboard tubes make perfect rockets. So, use your imagination!

Write **F** next to each fact and **O** next to each opinion.

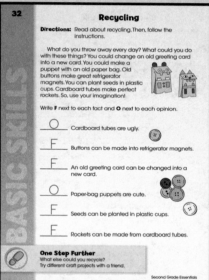

O __ Cardboard tubes are ugly.
F __ Buttons can be made into refrigerator magnets.
F __ An old greeting card can be changed into a new card.
O __ Paper-bag puppets are cute.
F __ Seeds can be planted in plastic cups.
F __ Rockets can be made from cardboard tubes.

One Step Further
What else could you recycle? Try different craft projects with a friend.

Second Grade Essentials

An Owl Story

33

Directions: Read the story. Then, follow the instructions.

My name is Owen Owl, and I am a bird. I go to Nocturnal School. Our teacher is Mr. Screech Owl. In his class, I learned that owls are birds and can sleep all day and hunt at night. Some of us live in nests in trees. In North America, it is against the law to harm owls. I like being an owl!

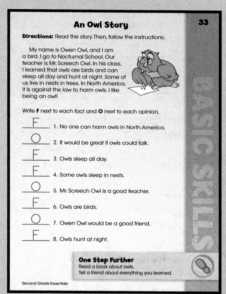

Write **F** next to each fact and **O** next to each opinion.

F __ 1. No one can harm owls in North America.
O __ 2. It would be great if owls could talk.
F __ 3. Owls sleep all day.
F __ 4. Some owls sleep in nests.
O __ 5. Mr. Screech Owl is a good teacher.
F __ 6. Owls are birds.
O __ 7. Owen Owl would be a good friend.
F __ 8. Owls hunt at night.

One Step Further
Read a book about owls. Tell a friend about everything you learned.

Second Grade Essentials

Henrietta the Humpback

34

Directions: Read the story. Then, follow the instructions.

My name is Henrietta, and I am a humpback whale. I live in cold seas in the summer and warm seas in the winter. My long flippers are used to move forward and backward. I like to eat fish. Sometimes, I show off by leaping out of the water. Would you like to be a humpback whale?

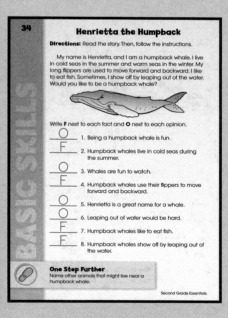

Write **F** next to each fact and **O** next to each opinion.

O __ 1. Being a humpback whale is fun.
F __ 2. Humpback whales live in cold seas during the summer.
O __ 3. Whales are fun to watch.
F __ 4. Humpback whales use their flippers to move forward and backward.
O __ 5. Henrietta is a great name for a whale.
O __ 6. Leaping out of water would be hard.
F __ 7. Humpback whales like to eat fish.
F __ 8. Humpback whales show off by leaping out of the water.

One Step Further
Name other animals that might live near a humpback whale.

Second Grade Essentials

Outdoor/Indoor Games

35

Classifying is putting things that are alike into groups.

Directions: Draw an **X** on the games you can play indoors. Circle the objects used for outdoor games.

One Step Further
Outdoor games are active. Indoor games are quiet. Which do you like best?

Second Grade Essentials

226

36

Classifying

Directions: Write each word from the word box on the correct line.

baby	goose	family	policeman
uncle	whale	kangaroo	
donkey	grandfather	fox	

people   **animals**

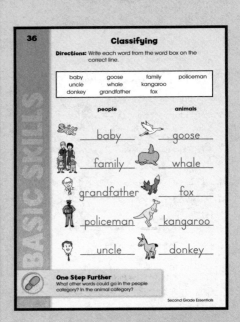

people	animals
baby	goose
family	whale
grandfather	fox
policeman	kangaroo
uncle	donkey

One Step Further
What other words could go in the people category? In the animal category?

Second Grade Essentials

37

Animals

Directions: Use a red crayon to circle the names of three animals that would make good pets. Use a blue crayon to circle the names of three wild animals. Use an orange crayon to circle the two animals that live on a farm.

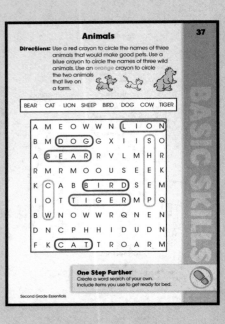

BEAR	CAT	LION	SHEEP	BIRD	DOG	COW	TIGER

```
A M E O W W N L I O N
B M D O G G X I I S O
A B E A R R V L M H R
R M R M O O U S E E K
K C A B B I R D S E M
I O T T I G E R M P Q
B W N O W W R Q N E N
D N C P H H I D U D N
F K C A T T R O A R M
```

One Step Further
Create a word search of your own. Include items you use to get ready for bed.

Second Grade Essentials

38

Animal Habitats

Directions: Read the article. Then, write each animal's name under **Water** or **Land** to tell where it lives.

Animals live in different habitats. A habitat is the place of an animal's natural home. Many animals live on land and others live in water. Most animals that live in water breathe with gills. Animals that live on land breathe with lungs.

fish	shrimp	giraffe	dog
cat	eel	whale	horse
bear	deer	shark	jellyfish

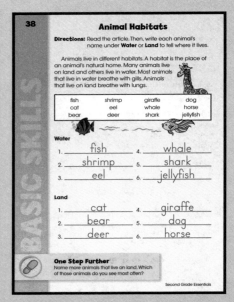

Water
1. fish   4. whale
2. shrimp   5. shark
3. eel   6. jellyfish

Land
1. cat   4. giraffe
2. bear   5. dog
3. deer   6. horse

One Step Further
Name more animals that live on land. Which of those animals do you see most often?

Second Grade Essentials

39

Cows Give Us Milk

Directions: Read the article. Answer the questions.

Cows live on farms. The farmer milks the cow to get milk. Many things are made from milk. We make ice cream, sour cream, cottage cheese, and butter from milk. Butter is fun to make! You can learn to make your own butter. First, you need cream. Put the cream in a jar and shake it. Then, you need to pour off the liquid. Next, you put the butter in a bowl. Add a little salt and stir! Finally, spread it on crackers and eat!

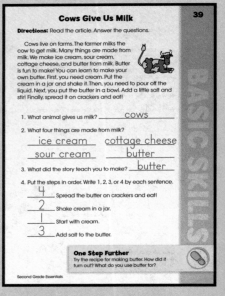

1. What animal gives us milk? ___cows___

2. What four things are made from milk?
   ice cream   cottage cheese
   sour cream   butter

3. What did the story teach you to make? ___butter___

4. Put the steps in order. Write 1, 2, 3, or 4 by each sentence.
   _4_ Spread the butter on crackers and eat!
   _2_ Shake cream in a jar.
   _1_ Start with cream.
   _3_ Add salt to the butter.

One Step Further
Try the recipe for making butter. How did it turn out? What do you use butter for?

Second Grade Essentials

40

How to Treat a Ladybug

Directions: Read about how to treat ladybugs. Then, follow the instructions.

Ladybugs are shy. If you see a ladybug, sit very still. Hold out your arm. Maybe the ladybug will fly to you. If it does, talk softly. Do not touch it. It will fly away when it is ready.

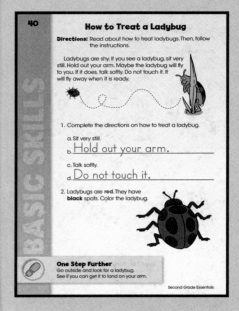

1. Complete the directions on how to treat a ladybug.
   a. Sit very still.
   b. Hold out your arm.
   c. Talk softly.
   d. Do not touch it.

2. Ladybugs are **red**. They have **black** spots. Color the ladybug.

One Step Further
Go outside and look for a ladybug. See if you can get it to land on your arm.

Second Grade Essentials

41

Find the Books

Directions: Use the clues to help the children find their books. Draw a line from each child's name to the correct book.

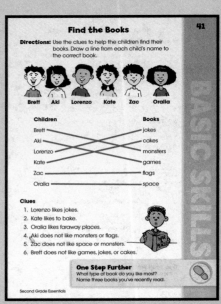

Brett   Aki   Lorenzo   Kate   Zac   Oralia

Children   **Books**
Brett   jokes
Aki   cakes
Lorenzo   monsters
Kate   games
Zac   flags
Oralia   space

Clues
1. Lorenzo likes jokes.
2. Kate likes to bake.
3. Oralia likes faraway places.
4. Aki does not like monsters or flags.
5. Zac does not like space or monsters.
6. Brett does not like games, jokes, or cakes.

One Step Further
What type of book do you like most? Name three books you've recently read.

Second Grade Essentials

Second Grade Essentials

ANSWER KEY

---

42 **Sports**

Children all over the world like to play sports. They like many different kinds of sports: football, soccer, basketball, softball, in-line skating, swimming, and more.

Directions: Read the clues. Draw dots on the chart to match the children with their sports.

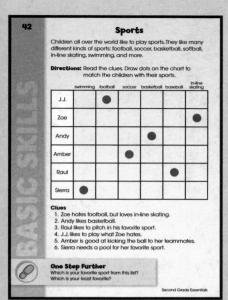

	swimming	football	soccer	basketball	baseball	in-line skating
J.J.		●				
Zoe						●
Andy				●		
Amber			●			
Raul					●	
Sierra	●					

Clues
1. Zoe hates football, but loves in-line skating.
2. Andy likes basketball.
3. Raul likes to pitch in his favorite sport.
4. J.J. likes to play what Zoe hates.
5. Amber is good at kicking the ball to her teammates.
6. Sierra needs a pool for her favorite sport.

One Step Further
Which is your favorite sport from this list?
Which is your least favorite?

Second Grade Essentials

---

44 **Batter Up!**

What did Bobby yell to the batter?

Directions: To find out, say the name of each picture. On the line, write the letter that you hear at the beginning of each picture.

H i t a

h o m e r u n!

One Step Further
Go outside and play baseball with a friend.
See how far you can hit the ball.

Second Grade Essentials

Tic-Tac-Toe **45**

Directions: Find the three pictures in each game whose names begin with the same sound. Draw a line through them.

One Step Further
Play a game of tic-tac-toe with a friend.
The winner gets to choose the next game.

Second Grade Essentials

---

46 **Consonant Blends**

Consonant blends are two or three consonant letters in a word whose sounds combine, or blend.

Example: br, fr, gr, pr, tr

Directions: Look at each picture. Say its name. Write the blend you hear at the beginning of each word.

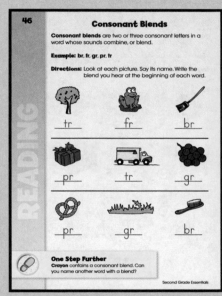

tr fr br

pr tr gr

pr gr br

One Step Further
Crayon contains a consonant blend. Can you name another word with a blend?

Second Grade Essentials

Blend Match-Up **47**

Directions: Say the name of each picture. Draw lines to match the pictures that have the same beginning blend.

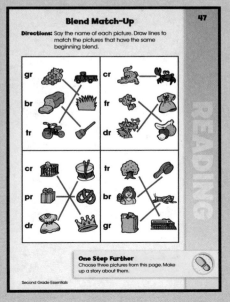

gr cr
br fr
tr dr

cr tr
pr br
dr gr

One Step Further
Choose three pictures from this page. Make up a story about them.

Second Grade Essentials

---

48 **Crown the King**

Directions: Write the beginning blend on the line. These words go across in the puzzle.

1. drum   3. grapes   5. crown

Directions: These words go down in the puzzle.

1. dress   2. green   4. cry

Can you write each word from above in the puzzle?

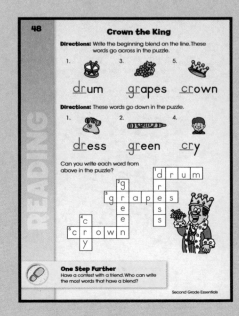

One Step Further
Have a contest with a friend. Who can write the most words that have a blend?

Second Grade Essentials

Second Grade Essentials

ANSWER KEY

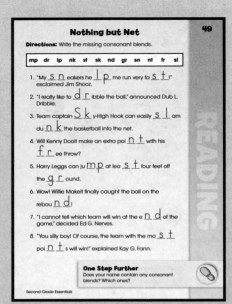

Nothing but Net

49

Directions: Write the missing consonant blends.

mp	dr	lp	nk	st	sk	nd	gr	sn	nt	fr	sl

1. "My **sn**eakers he**lp** me run very fa**st**!" exclaimed Jim Shooz.
2. "I really like to **dr**ibble the ball," announced Dub L. Dribble.
3. Team captain **Sk**y-High Hook can easily **sl**am du**nk** the basketball into the net.
4. Will Kenny Dooit make an extra poi**nt** with his **fr**ee throw?
5. Harry Leggs can ju**mp** at lea**st** four feet off the **gr**ound.
6. Wow! Willie Makeit finally caught the ball on the rebou**nd**!
7. "I cannot tell which team will win at the e**nd** of the game," decided Ed G. Nerves.
8. "You silly boy! Of course, the team with the mo**st** poi**nt**s will win!" explained Kay G. Fann.

READING

One Step Further
Does your name contain any consonant blends? Which ones?

Second Grade Essentials

Missing Digraphs

50

Directions: Fill in the circle beside the missing digraph in each word.

___ale	pea___	___ife
● wh ○ wr ○ ch	○ ck ○ th ● ch	● kn ○ ch ○ wr
___imp	**___ell**	**clo___**
○ ck ○ kn ● ch	○ ch ● sh ○ ck	● ck ○ ch ○ kn
___ite	**fi___**	**___orn**
○ kn ● wr ○ th	○ ch ● sh ○ th	● th ○ wr ○ ch

READING

One Step Further
Look at the digraphs that are not filled in. Name words using those digraphs.

Second Grade Essentials

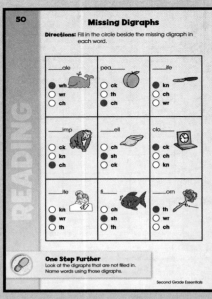

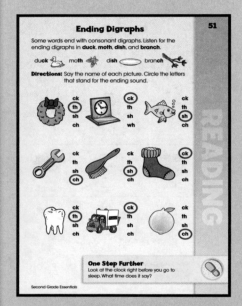

Ending Digraphs

51

Some words end with consonant digraphs. Listen for the ending digraphs in **duck**, **moth**, **dish**, and **branch**.

duck   moth   dish   branch

Directions: Say the name of each picture. Circle the letters that stand for the ending sound.

Picture	Choices	Circled
wreath	ck th sh ch	th
clock	ck th sh wh	ck
fish	ck th sh ch	sh
wrench	ck th sh ch	ch
brush	ck th sh ch	sh
sock	ck th sh ch	ck
tooth	ck th sh ch	th
truck	ck th sh ch	ck
peach	ck th sh ch	ch

READING

One Step Further
Look at the clock right before you go to sleep. What time does it say?

Second Grade Essentials

Silent Letters

52

Some words have letters you cannot hear at all, such as the **gh** in **night**, the **w** in **wrong**, the **l** in **walk**, the **k** in **knee**, the **b** in **climb**, and the **t** in **listen**.

Directions: Look at the words in the word box. Write the word under its picture. Underline the silent letters.

knife	light	calf	wrench	lamb	eight
wrist	whistle	comb	thumb	knob	knee

eight   wrist   knee   calf

lamb   knob   whistle   light

wrench   comb   thumb   knife

READING

One Step Further
Think of other words you know that have a silent letter. What are those words?

Second Grade Essentials

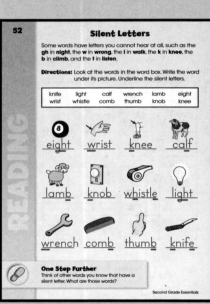

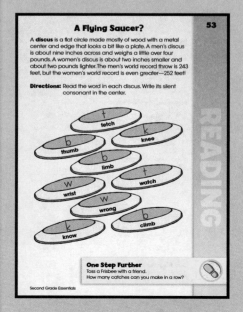

A Flying Saucer?

53

A **discus** is a flat circle made mostly of wood with a metal center and edge that looks a bit like a plate. A men's discus is about nine inches across and weighs a little over four pounds. A women's discus is about two inches smaller and about two pounds lighter. The men's world record throw is 243 feet, but the women's world record is even greater—252 feet!

Directions: Read the word in each discus. Write its silent consonant in the center.

Word	Silent consonant
fetch	t
knee	k
thumb	b
limb	b
watch	t
wrist	w
wrong	w
climb	b
know	k

READING

One Step Further
Toss a Frisbee with a friend.
How many catches can you make in a row?

Second Grade Essentials

Sounds of c and g

54

Consonants **c** and **g** each have two sounds. Listen for the soft **c** sound in **pencil**. Listen for the hard **c** sound in **cup**.

Listen for the soft **g** sound in **giant**. Listen for the hard **g** sound in **goat**. **C** and **g** usually have the soft sound when they are followed by **e**, **i**, or **y**.

Directions: Say the name of each picture. Listen for the sound of **c** or **g**. Then, read the words in each list. Circle the words that have that sound of **c** or **g**.

Hard c — cup	Soft c — pencil
(car) race city rice (cone) (can)	cage cane (face) (cent) (ice) cube
Hard g — goat	**Soft g — giant**
(good) magic (dragon) (gum) stage gentle	garden (gem) (page) (giraffe) gas gorilla

READING

One Step Further
List words that contain **c** or **g**.
Write whether those are hard or soft letters.

Second Grade Essentials

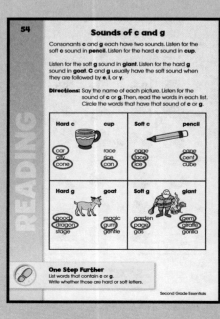

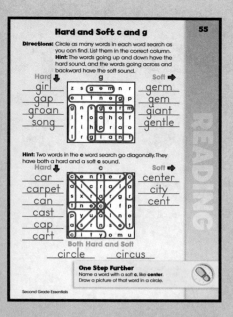

Hard and Soft c and g — 55

Directions: Circle as many words in each word search as you can find. List them in the correct column.
Hint: The words going up and down have the hard sound, and the words going across and backward have the soft sound.

Hard ↓   g   Soft ➡

girl / gap / groan / song

germ / gem / giant / gentle

Hint: Two words in the **c** word search go diagonally. They have both a hard and a soft **c** sound.

Hard ↓   c   Soft ➡

car / carpet / can / cast / cap / cart

center / city / cent

Both Hard and Soft
circle   circus

One Step Further
Name a word with a soft **c**, like **center**. Draw a picture of that word in a circle.

Second Grade Essentials

Kick It In! — 56

Directions: Write a vowel to complete each word below.

n e t
p a ss
s o cks
r u n
k i ck

One Step Further
Kick a soccer ball outside. Say a word with a different vowel sound with each kick.

Second Grade Essentials

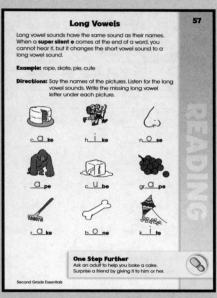

Long Vowels — 57

Long vowel sounds have the same sound as their names. When a **super silent e** comes at the end of a word, you cannot hear it, but it changes the short vowel sound to a long vowel sound.

Example: rope, skate, pie, cute

Directions: Say the names of the pictures. Listen for the long vowel sounds. Write the missing long vowel letter under each picture.

c a ke   h i ke   n o se

a pe   c u be   gr a pe

r a ke   b o ne   k i te

One Step Further
Ask an adult to help you bake a cake. Surprise a friend by giving it to him or her.

Second Grade Essentials

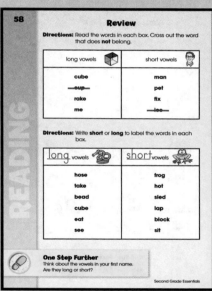

Review — 58

Directions: Read the words in each box. Cross out the word that does **not** belong.

long vowels	short vowels
cube	man
~~cup~~	pet
rake	fix
me	~~ice~~

Directions: Write **short** or **long** to label the words in each box.

long vowels	short vowels
hose	frog
take	hot
bead	sled
cube	lap
eat	block
see	sit

One Step Further
Think about the vowels in your first name. Are they long or short?

Second Grade Essentials

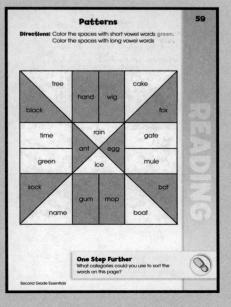

Patterns — 59

Directions: Color the spaces with short vowel words green. Color the spaces with long vowel words.

tree			cake
hand	wig	
black			fox
time	rain		gate
	ant	egg	
green	ice		mule
sock			bat
name	gum	mop	boat

One Step Further
What categories could you use to sort the words on this page?

Second Grade Essentials

Tricky ar — 60

When **r** follows a vowel, it changes the vowel's sound. Listen for the **ar** sound in **star**.

Directions: Color the pictures whose names have the **ar** sound.

One Step Further
Draw 10 stars. Write a word that starts with the letter **s** on each star.

Second Grade Essentials

READING
ANSWER KEY

230

ANSWER KEY

Write ar or or — 61
Listen for the **or** sound in **horn**.

Directions: Write **ar** or **or** to complete each word.

- th**orn**
- c**ar**t
- f**or**ty
- st**or**k
- c**or**n
- h**ar**p
- **ar**m
- st**ar**
- p**or**ch

One Step Further
Draw a picture of a flower in a jar. Label the parts of the flower, including the thorns.

Second Grade Essentials

Mix and Match — 62
The letters **ur**, **er**, and **ir** all have the same sound. Listen for the vowel sound in **surf**, **fern**, and **girl**.

surf   fern   girl

Directions: Draw a line from each word to the picture it names.

- herd
- turkey
- clerk
- thirty
- purse
- bird

One Step Further
Name 10 friends or family members. Then, write them out in ABC order.

Second Grade Essentials

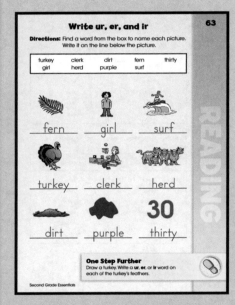

Write ur, er, and ir — 63
Directions: Find a word from the box to name each picture. Write it on the line below the picture.

| turkey | clerk | dirt | fern | thirty |
| girl | herd | purple | surf | |

- fern
- girl
- surf
- turkey
- clerk
- herd
- dirt
- purple
- thirty

One Step Further
Draw a turkey. Write a **ur**, **er**, or **ir** word on each of the turkey's feathers.

Second Grade Essentials

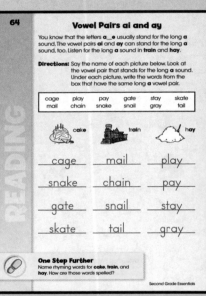

Vowel Pairs ai and ay — 64
You know that the letters **a__e** usually stand for the long **a** sound. The vowel pairs **ai** and **ay** can stand for the long **a** sound, too. Listen for the long **a** sound in **train** and **hay**.

Directions: Say the name of each picture below. Look at the vowel pair that stands for the long **a** sound. Under each picture, write the words from the box that have the same long **a** vowel pair.

| cage | play | pay | gate | stay | skate |
| mail | chain | snake | snail | gray | tail |

cake — train — hay

cage	mail	play
snake	chain	pay
gate	snail	stay
skate	tail	gray

One Step Further
Name rhyming words for **cake**, **train**, and **hay**. How are those words spelled?

Second Grade Essentials

Vowel Pairs oa and ow — 65
You know that the letters **o__e** and **oe** usually stand for the long **o** sound. The vowel pairs **oa** and **ow** can stand for the long **o** sound, too. Listen for the long **o** sound in **road** and **snow**.

Directions: Find and circle eight long **o** words. The words may go across or down. Beside each picture, write the words that use the same long **o** vowel pair.

```
Z L I A C R
B O C R O W
S W R J A G
O G O A L R
A L A G X O
P Y K N O W
```

- road: soap, goal, coal, croak
- snow: low, know, grow, row

One Step Further
Walk or ride your bike down the road you live on. What do you pass?

Second Grade Essentials

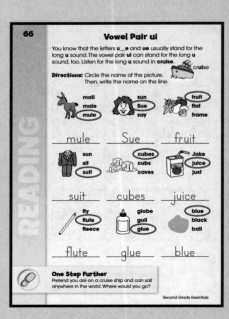

Vowel Pair ui — 66
You know that the letters **u__e** and **ue** usually stand for the long **u** sound. The vowel pair **ui** can stand for the long **u** sound, too. Listen for the long **u** sound in **cruise**.

Directions: Circle the name of the picture. Then, write the name on the line.

- mail / male / **mule** → mule
- sun / **Sue** / say → Sue
- **fruit** / flat / frame → fruit
- sun / sit / **suit** → suit
- **cubes** / cubs / caves → cubes
- Jake / **juice** / just → juice
- fly / **flute** / fleece → flute
- globe / gull / **glue** → glue
- **blue** / black / ball → blue

One Step Further
Pretend you are on a cruise ship and can sail anywhere in the world. Where would you go?

Second Grade Essentials

Second Grade Essentials

Vowel Pair ie — 67

You know that the letters i_e usually stand for the long i sound. The vowel pair ie can stand for the long i sound, too. Listen for the long i sound in **butterflies**.

Directions: Write i_e or ie to complete each word.

butterflies

dime   tie   flies

five   knife   tried

pie   lie   kite

One Step Further
Choose one i_e word and one ie word. Draw each picture here.

Second Grade Essentials

Vowel Pair ea — 68

Some vowel pairs can stand for more than one sound. The vowel pair **ea** has the sound of long **e** in **team** and short **e** in **head**.

team   head

Directions: Say the name of each picture. Listen for the sound that **ea** stands for. Circle **Long e** or **Short e**. Then, color the pictures whose names have the short **e** sound.

Row 1: (Long e) Short e   Long e (Short e)   (Long e) Short e
Row 2: Long e (Short e)   Long e (Short e)   (Long e) Short e
Row 3: Long e (Short e)   (Long e) Short e   Long e (Short e)

One Step Further
Talk about a team that you have been on recently. What was your role on the team?

Second Grade Essentials

Vowel Pair oo — 69

Listen for the difference between the sound of the vowel pair **oo** in **moon** and its sound in **book**.

moon   book

Directions: Say the name of the picture. Circle the picture of the moon or the book to show the sound of vowel pair **oo**.

One Step Further
What is the best book you've read recently? What did you like about it?

Second Grade Essentials

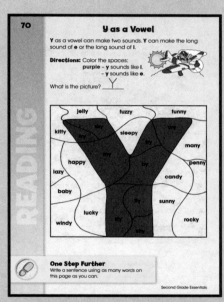

Y as a Vowel — 70

Y as a vowel can make two sounds. Y can make the long sound of **e** or the long sound of **i**.

Directions: Color the spaces:
purple - **y** sounds like **i**.
   - **y** sounds like **e**.

What is the picture? Y

(Words: jelly, fuzzy, funny, kitty, sly, sleepy, dry, fry, many, happy, fry, by, penny, lazy, candy, baby, cry, sunny, lucky, fly, rocky, windy, shy, why)

One Step Further
Write a sentence using as many words on this page as you can.

Second Grade Essentials

A Fork in the Road — 71

Directions: Write the words below on the correct "road."

sky	jelly	try	kitty	dry	my
fry	cry	funny	happy	lazy	baby
candy	by	sleepy	many	penny	
sly	fuzzy	shy	fly	why	

Y sounds like long e.	Y sounds like long i.
candy	sky
jelly	fry
fuzzy	sly
funny	cry
sleepy	by
kitty	try
happy	shy
many	fly
lazy	dry
penny	why
baby	my

One Step Further
Draw a road that takes you across a map of the United States. Label the states you pass.

Second Grade Essentials

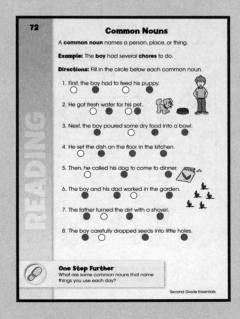

Common Nouns — 72

A **common noun** names a person, place, or thing.

Example: The **boy** had several **chores** to do.

Directions: Fill in the circle below each common noun.

1. First, the boy had to feed his puppy.
   ● ○
2. He got fresh water for his pet.
   ○ ●
3. Next, the boy poured some dry food into a bowl.
   ● ○ ●
4. He set the dish on the floor in the kitchen.
   ● ● ●
5. Then, he called his dog to come to dinner.
   ○ ●
6. The boy and his dad worked in the garden.
   ● ● ●
7. The father turned the dirt with a shovel.
   ● ○ ●
8. The boy carefully dropped seeds into little holes.
   ● ○ ● ●

One Step Further
What are some common nouns that name things you use each day?

Second Grade Essentials

231

ANSWER KEY

Second Grade Essentials

Proper Nouns   73

A **proper noun** names a specific or certain person, place, or thing. A proper noun always begins with a capital letter.

Example: **Becky** flew to **St. Louis** in a **Boeing 747**.

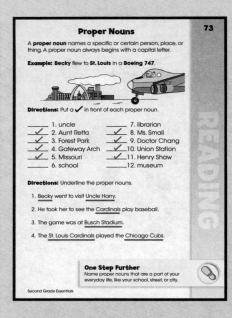

Directions: Put a ✔ in front of each proper noun.

____ 1. uncle
✔ 2. Aunt Retta
✔ 3. Forest Park
✔ 4. Gateway Arch
✔ 5. Missouri
____ 6. school
✔ 7. librarian
✔ 8. Ms. Small
✔ 9. Doctor Chang
✔ 10. Union Station
✔ 11. Henry Shaw
____ 12. museum

Directions: Underline the proper nouns.

1. Becky went to visit Uncle Harry.

2. He took her to see the Cardinals play baseball.

3. The game was at Busch Stadium.

4. The St. Louis Cardinals played the Chicago Cubs.

One Step Further
Name proper nouns that are a part of your everyday life, like your school, street, or city.

Second Grade Essentials

Singular Nouns   74

A **singular noun** names one person, place, or thing.

Example: My **mother** unlocked the old **trunk** in the **attic**.

Directions: If the noun is singular, draw a line from it to the trunk. If the noun is **not** singular, draw an **X** on the word.

teddy bear   hammer   picture   sweater
bonnet   letters   seashells   fiddle
kite   ring   feather   boots
postcard   crayon   doll   glasses
bugs   bus   bicycle   blanket

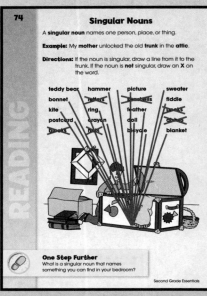

One Step Further
What is a singular noun that names something you can find in your bedroom?

Second Grade Essentials

Plural Nouns   75

A **plural noun** names more than one person, place, or thing.

Example: Some **dinosaurs** ate **plants** in **swamps**.

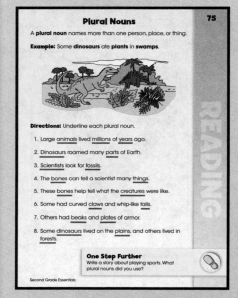

Directions: Underline each plural noun.

1. Large animals lived millions of years ago.

2. Dinosaurs roamed many parts of Earth.

3. Scientists look for fossils.

4. The bones can tell a scientist many things.

5. These bones help tell what the creatures were like.

6. Some had curved claws and whip-like tails.

7. Others had beaks and plates of armor.

8. Some dinosaurs lived on the plains, and others lived in forests.

One Step Further
Write a story about playing sports. What plural nouns did you use?

Second Grade Essentials

Action Verbs   76

A **verb** is a word that can show action.

Example: I **jump**.   He **kicks**.   He **walked**.

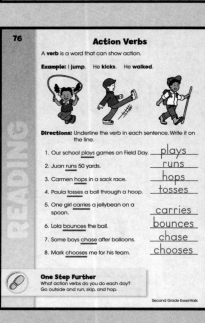

Directions: Underline the verb in each sentence. Write it on the line.

1. Our school plays games on Field Day.   plays

2. Juan runs 50 yards.   runs

3. Carmen hops in a sack race.   hops

4. Paula tosses a ball through a hoop.   tosses

5. One girl carries a jellybean on a spoon.   carries

6. Lola bounces the ball.   bounces

7. Some boys chase after balloons.   chase

8. Mark chooses me for his team.   chooses

One Step Further
What action verbs do you do each day? Go outside and run, skip, and hop.

Second Grade Essentials

Verbs   77

Directions: Circle the words in the puzzle. The words go across, down, and diagonally.

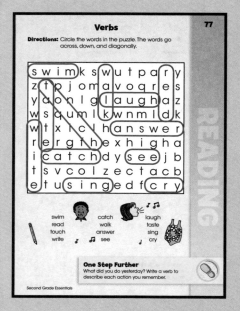

swim   catch   laugh
read   walk   taste
touch   answer   sing
write   see   cry

One Step Further
What did you do yesterday? Write a verb to describe each action you remember.

Second Grade Essentials

Linking Verbs   78

A **linking verb** does not show action. Instead, it links the subject with a word in the predicate. **Am**, **is**, **are**, **was**, and **were** are **linking verbs**.

Example: Many people **are** collectors.
(**Are** connects **people** and **collectors**.)
The collection **was** large.
(**Was** connects **collection** and **large**.)

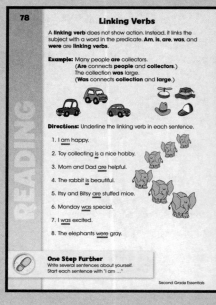

Directions: Underline the linking verb in each sentence.

1. I am happy.

2. Toy collecting is a nice hobby.

3. Mom and Dad are helpful.

4. The rabbit is beautiful.

5. Itsy and Bitsy are stuffed mice.

6. Monday was special.

7. I was excited.

8. The elephants were gray.

One Step Further
Write several sentences about yourself. Start each sentence with "I am ..."

Second Grade Essentials

ANSWER KEY

Irregular Verbs | 79

Verbs that do not add **ed** to show what happened in the past are called **irregular verbs**.

Example:
Present	Past
run, runs	ran
fall, falls	fell

Jim **ran** past our house yesterday.
He **fell** over a wagon on the sidewalk.

Directions: Fill in the verbs that tell what happened in the past in the chart. The first one is done for you.

Present	Past
hear, hears	heard
draw, draws	drew
do, does	did
give, gives	gave
sell, sells	sold
come, comes	came
fly, flies	flew
build, builds	built

One Step Further
Think of something you did yesterday.
Will you do the same thing again today?

Second Grade Essentials

Is, Are, and Am | 80

Is, **are**, and **am** are special action words that tell us something is happening now.

Use **am** with I. **Example:** I **am**.
Use **is** to tell about one person or thing. **Example:** He **is**.
Use **are** to tell about more than one. **Example:** We **are**.
Use **are** with **you**. **Example:** You **are**.

Directions: Write **is**, **are**, or **am** in the sentences below.

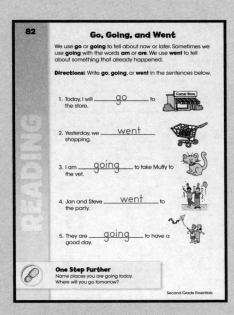

1. My friends _____are_____ helping me build a tree house.

2. It _____is_____ in my backyard.

3. We _____are_____ using hammers, wood, and nails.

4. It _____is_____ a very hard job.

5. I _____am_____ lucky to have good friends.

One Step Further
Write a sentence about you and two friends.
What action word did you use?

Second Grade Essentials

Was and Were | 81

Was and **were** tell us about something that already happened.

Use **was** to tell about one person or thing. **Example:** I **was**, he **was**. Use **were** to tell about more than one person or thing or when using the word **you**. **Example:** We **were**, you **were**.

Directions: Write **was** or **were** in each sentence.

1. Lily _____was_____ eight years old on her birthday.

2. Tim and Steve _____were_____ happy to be at the party.

3. Megan _____was_____ too shy to sing "Happy Birthday."

4. Ben _____was_____ sorry he dropped his cake.

5. All of the children _____were_____ happy to be invited.

One Step Further
Tell a story about something that happened yesterday. What were you doing?

Second Grade Essentials

Go, Going, and Went | 82

We use **go** or **going** to tell about now or later. Sometimes we use **going** with the words **am** or **are**. We use **went** to tell about something that already happened.

Directions: Write **go**, **going**, or **went** in the sentences below.

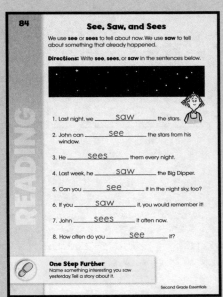

1. Today, I will _____go_____ to the store.

2. Yesterday, we _____went_____ shopping.

3. I am _____going_____ to take Muffy to the vet.

4. Jan and Steve _____went_____ to the party.

5. They are _____going_____ to have a good day.

One Step Further
Name places you are going today.
Where will you go tomorrow?

Second Grade Essentials

Have, Has, and Had | 83

We use **have** and **has** to tell about something that already happened. We use **had** to tell about something that already happened.

Directions: Write **has**, **have**, or **had** in the sentences below.

1. We _____have_____ three cats at home.

2. Ginger _____has_____ brown fur.

3. Bucky and Charlie _____have_____ gray fur.

4. My friend Tom _____had_____ one cat, but it died.

5. Tom _____has_____ a new cat now.

One Step Further
Name something you have. Name something you had yesterday, but not today.

Second Grade Essentials

See, Saw, and Sees | 84

We use **see** or **sees** to tell about now. We use **saw** to tell about something that already happened.

Directions: Write **see**, **sees**, or **saw** in the sentences below.

1. Last night, we _____saw_____ the stars.

2. John can _____see_____ the stars from his window.

3. He _____sees_____ them every night.

4. Last week, he _____saw_____ the Big Dipper.

5. Can you _____see_____ it in the night sky, too?

6. If you _____saw_____ it, you would remember it!

7. John _____sees_____ it often now.

8. How often do you _____see_____ it?

One Step Further
Name something interesting you saw yesterday. Tell a story about it.

Second Grade Essentials

Eat, Eats, and Ate

We use **eat** or **eats** to tell about now. We use **ate** to tell about what already happened.

Directions: Write eat, eats, or ate in the sentences below.

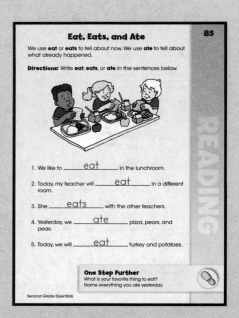

1. We like to _____eat_____ in the lunchroom.

2. Today, my teacher will _____eat_____ in a different room.

3. She _____eats_____ with the other teachers.

4. Yesterday, we _____ate_____ pizza, pears, and peas.

5. Today, we will _____eat_____ turkey and potatoes.

One Step Further
What is your favorite thing to eat? Name everything you ate yesterday.

Second Grade Essentials

85

READING

86

Adjectives

An **adjective** is a word that describes a noun. It tells **how many**, **what kind**, or **which one**.

Example: Yolanda has a **tasty** lunch.

Directions: Color each space that has an adjective. Do not color the other spaces.

One Step Further
What adjectives would you use to describe your school? Name as many as you can.

Second Grade Essentials

READING

Better Sentences

Directions: Describing words like adjectives can make a better sentence. Write a word on each line to make the sentences more interesting. Draw pictures of your sentences.

1. The skater won a medal.
The _____ skater won a _____ medal.

2. The jewels were in the safe.
The _____ jewels were in the _____ safe.

3. The airplane flew through the storm.
The _____ airplane flew through the storm. Answers will vary.

4. A firefighter rushed into the house.
A _____ firefighter rushed into the _____ house.

5. The detective hid behind the tree.
The _____ detective hid behind the _____ tree.

Drawings will vary.

1.	2.
3.	4.	5.

One Step Further
Write a sentence. Then, make it better by adding adjectives to the sentence.

Second Grade Essentials

87

READING

88

Compound Words

Directions: Read the sentences. Fill in the blank with a compound word from the box.

raincoat	bedroom	lunchbox	hallway	sandbox

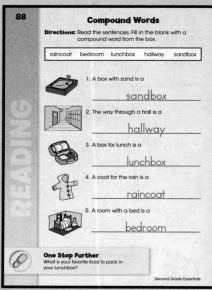

1. A box with sand is a
_____sandbox_____

2. The way through a hall is a
_____hallway_____

3. A box for lunch is a
_____lunchbox_____

4. A coat for the rain is a
_____raincoat_____

5. A room with a bed is a
_____bedroom_____

One Step Further
What is your favorite food to pack in your lunchbox?

Second Grade Essentials

READING

Word Magic

Maggie Magician announced, "One plus one equals one!" The audience giggled. So, Maggie put two words into a hat and waved her magic wand. When she reached into the hat, Maggie pulled out one word and a picture. "See," said Maggie, "I was right!"

Directions: Use the word box to help you write a compound word for each picture below.

ball	rain	shirt	fish	book	basket
bow	box	light	cup	tail	worm
door	star	bell	shoe	foot	
lace	stool	sun	mail	cake	

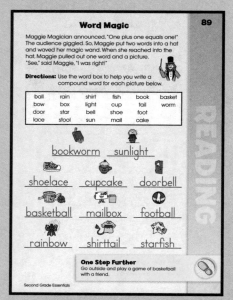

bookworm   sunlight

shoelace   cupcake   doorbell

basketball   mailbox   football

rainbow   shirttail   starfish

One Step Further
Go outside and play a game of basketball with a friend.

Second Grade Essentials

89

READING

90

Compound Fun

Directions: Match each word in the box with a word in the puzzle to make a new word.

cake	shine	knob	room
port	shore	ball	fish

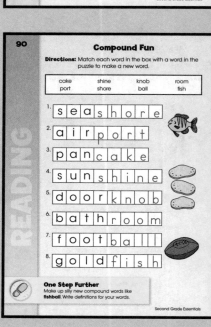

1. s e a s h o r e
2. a i r p o r t
3. p a n c a k e
4. s u n s h i n e
5. d o o r k n o b
6. b a t h r o o m
7. f o o t b a l l
8. g o l d f i s h

One Step Further
Make up silly new compound words like **fishball**. Write definitions for your words.

Second Grade Essentials

READING

Tasty Compounds — 91

Directions: Circle the words in the puzzle. The words go across, down, and diagonally.

p	e	p	p	e	r	m	i	n	t	x	y	a
o	g	g	r	a	p	e	f	r	u	i	t	z
p	t	u	j	k	n	s	e	a	f	o	o	d
c	v	p	l	s	q	c	u	p	c	a	k	e
o	w	e	m	o	r	o	a	t	m	e	a	l
r	i	a	n	b	r	e	a	k	f	a	s	t
n	g	n	p	b	l	u	e	b	e	r	r	y
f	h	u	e	f	r	u	i	t	c	a	k	e
w	a	t	e	r	m	e	l	o	n	b	d	c

watermelon   fruitcake   peppermint
popcorn   cupcake   blueberry
pancake   breakfast   grapefruit
oatmeal   peanut   seafood

One Step Further
Plan a special meal for your mom or dad. Write the menu.

Second Grade Essentials

Contractions — 92

A **contraction** is a word made up of two words joined together with one or more letters left out. An **apostrophe** is used in place of the missing letters.

Example: I am—**I'm**
do not—**don't**
that is—**that's**

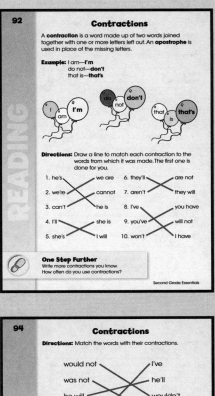

Directions: Draw a line to match each contraction to the words from which it was made. The first one is done for you.

1. he's — he is
2. we're — we are
3. can't — cannot
4. I'll — I will
5. she's — she is
6. they'll — they will
7. aren't — are not
8. I've — I have
9. you've — you have
10. won't — will not

One Step Further
Write more contractions you know. How often do you use contractions?

Second Grade Essentials

Contractions — 93

Contractions are a short way to write two words, such as **isn't**, **I've**, and **weren't**.

Example: it is—**it's**

Directions: Draw a line from each word pair to its contraction.

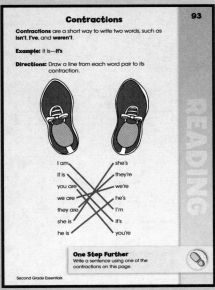

I am — I'm
it is — it's
you are — you're
we are — we're
they are — they're
she is — she's
he is — he's

One Step Further
Write a sentence using one of the contractions on this page.

Second Grade Essentials

Contractions — 94

Directions: Match the words with their contractions.

would not — wouldn't
was not — wasn't
he will — he'll
could not — couldn't
I have — I've

Directions: Make the words at the end of each line into contractions to complete the sentences.

1. He _didn't_ know the answer.   **did not**
2. _It's_ a long way home.   **It is**
3. _Here's_ my house.   **Here is**
4. _We're_ not going to school today.   **We are**

One Step Further
Write a story. How many contractions can you use?

Second Grade Essentials

Something Is Missing! — 95

Directions: Write the correct contraction for each set of words. Then, circle the letter that was left out when the contraction was made.

| doesn't | it's | didn't | who's | he's |
| don't | aren't | she's | that's | isn't |

1. he i~~s~~   _he's_
2. are n~~o~~t   _aren't_
3. do n~~o~~t   _don't_
4. who i~~s~~   _who's_
5. is n~~o~~t   _isn't_
6. did n~~o~~t   _didn't_
7. it i~~s~~   _it's_
8. she i~~s~~   _she's_
9. does n~~o~~t   _doesn't_
10. that i~~s~~   _that's_

Directions: Write the missing contraction on the line.

1. _She's_ on her way to school.
2. There _isn't_ enough time to finish the story.
3. Do you think _it's_ too long?
4. We _aren't_ going to the party.
5. Donna _didn't_ like the movie.
6. _Who's_ going to try for a part in the play?
7. Bob said _he's_ going to run in the big race.
8. They _don't_ know how to bake a cake.
9. Tom _doesn't_ want to go skating on Saturday.
10. Look, _that's_ where they found the lost watch.

One Step Further
Write a letter to a friend. Use as many contractions as you can.

Second Grade Essentials

Prefixes — 96

Directions: Change the meaning of the sentences by adding prefixes to the **bold** words.

The boy was **lucky** because he guessed the answer **correctly**.

The boy was (un) _unlucky_ because he guessed the answer (in) _incorrectly_

When Mary **behaved**, she felt **happy**.

When Mary (mis) _misbehaved_ she felt (un) _unhappy_

Mike wore his jacket **buttoned** because the dance was **formal**.

Mike wore his jacket (un) _unbuttoned_ because the dance was (in) _informal_

One Step Further
Tell a story about a time you misbehaved. What happened after you misbehaved?

Second Grade Essentials

ANSWER KEY

236

ANSWER KEY

Page 97 — Prefixes: The Three Rs

Prefixes are syllables added to the beginning of words that change their meaning. The prefix **re** means "again."

Directions: Read the story. Then, follow the instructions.

Kim wants to find ways she can save Earth. She studies the "three Rs"—reduce, reuse, and recycle. **Reduce** means to make less. Both **reuse** and **recycle** mean to use again.

Add **re** to the beginning of each word below. Use the new words to complete the sentences.

__re__ build   __re__ write   __re__ tell
__re__ read   __re__ fill   __re__ run

1. The race was a tie, so Dawn and Kathy had to __rerun__ it.
2. The block wall fell down, so Simon had to __rebuild__ it.
3. The water bottle was empty, so Luna had to __refill__ it.
4. Javier wrote a good story, but he wanted to __rewrite__ it to make it better.
5. The teacher told a story, and the students had to __retell__ it.
6. Toni didn't understand the directions, so she had to __reread__ them.

One Step Further
Do you recycle? Name ways you can reuse different objects.

Second Grade Essentials

Page 98 — Suffixes

A **suffix** is a syllable that is added at the end of a word to change its meaning.

Directions: Add the suffixes to the root words to make new words. Use your new words to complete the sentences.

help + ful = __helpful__
build + er = __builder__
talk + ed = __talked__
love + ly = __lovely__
loud + er = __louder__

1. My mother __talked__ to my teacher about my homework.
2. The radio was __louder__ than the television.
3. Sally is always __helpful__ to her mother.
4. A __builder__ put a new garage on our house.
5. The flowers are __lovely__.

One Step Further
Describe ways you have been helpful to your friends and family.

Page 99 — Suffixes

Directions: Write a word from the word box next to its root word.

coming	visited	running	carried	swimming
lived	hurried	rained	sitting	racing

run __running__   come __coming__
live __lived__   carry __carried__
hurry __hurried__   race __racing__
swim __swimming__   rain __rained__
visit __visited__   sit __sitting__

Directions: Write a word from the word box to finish each sentence.

1. I __visited__ my grandmother during vacation.
2. Mary went __swimmimg__ at the lake with her cousin.
3. Jim __carried__ the heavy package for his mother.
4. It __rained__ and stormed all weekend.
5. Cars go very fast when they are __racing__.

One Step Further
Write a sentence about something that happened yesterday. Use the suffix **ed**.

Second Grade Essentials

Page 100 — Use the Clues

Context clues can help you figure out words you do not know. Read the words around the new word. Think of a word that makes sense.

Kate swam in a _____?

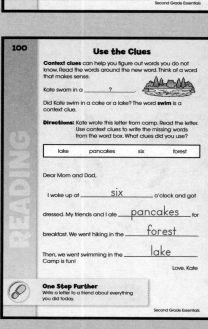

Did Kate swim in a cake or a lake? The word **swim** is a context clue.

Directions: Kate wrote this letter from camp. Read the letter. Use context clues to write the missing words from the word box. What clues did you use?

lake	pancakes	six	forest

Dear Mom and Dad,

I woke up at __six__ o'clock and got dressed. My friends and I ate __pancakes__ for breakfast. We went hiking in the __forest__. Then, we went swimming in the __lake__. Camp is fun!

Love, Kate

One Step Further
Write a letter to a friend about everything you did today.

Second Grade Essentials

Page 101 — Context Clues in Action

Directions: Read the story. Use context clues to figure out the meanings of the **bold** words. Draw a line from the word to its meaning. The first one is done for you.

Jack has a plan. He wants to take his parents out to lunch to show that he **appreciates** all the nice things they do for him. His sister Jessica will go, too, so she won't feel left out. Jack is **thrifty**. He saves the **allowance** he earns for doing **chores** around the house. So far, Jack has saved 10 dollars. He needs only five dollars more. He is excited about paying the check himself. He will feel like an **adult**.

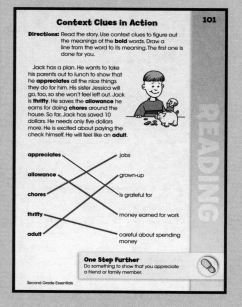

appreciates — jobs
allowance — grown-up
chores — is grateful for
thrifty — money earned for work
adult — careful about spending money

One Step Further
Do something to show that you appreciate a friend or family member.

Second Grade Essentials

Page 103 — Character

First, authors must decide who their main character is going to be. Next, they decide what their main character looks like. Then, they reveal the character's personality by:

what the character does
what the character says

Directions: Answer the questions about the story you just read.

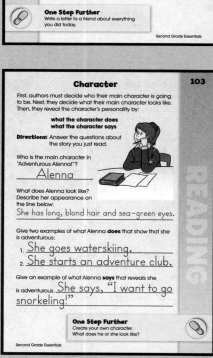

Who is the main character in "Adventurous Alenna"?
__Alenna__

What does Alenna look like? Describe her appearance on the line below:
She has long, blond hair and sea-green eyes.

Give two examples of what Alenna **does** that show that she is adventurous.
1. She goes waterskiing.
2. She starts an adventure club.

Give an example of what Alenna **says** that reveals she is adventurous. She says, "I want to go snorkeling."

One Step Further
Create your own character. What does he or she look like?

Second Grade Essentials

Second Grade Essentials

Setting — Place

104

Every story has a **setting**. The setting is the **place** where the story happens. Think of a place that you know well. It could be your room, your kitchen, your backyard, your classroom, or an imaginary place.

Directions: Brainstorm some words and ideas about that place. Think about what you see, hear, smell, taste, or feel in that place.

Brainstorm your ideas for a setting below:

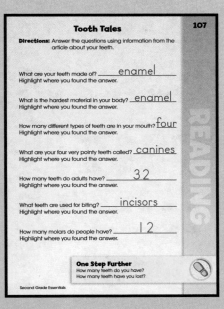

see
hear
smell
taste
touch

_____
_____
_____
Answers will vary.
_____
_____
_____
_____
_____

Where are we? _____

One Step Further
With a friend, brainstorm ideas for a play.
Act out your play for your family members.

Second Grade Essentials

Setting — Time

105

The **setting** is the **place** where the story happens. The setting is also the **time** in which the story happens. A reader needs to know **when** the story is happening. Does it take place at night? On a sunny day? In the future? During the winter?

Time can be:

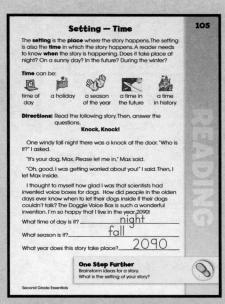

time of day | a holiday | a season of the year | a time in the future | a time in history

Directions: Read the following story. Then, answer the questions.

Knock, Knock!

One windy fall night there was a knock at the door. "Who is it?" I asked.

"It's your dog, Max. Please let me in," Max said.

"Oh, good. I was getting worried about you!" I said. Then, I let Max inside.

I thought to myself how glad I was that scientists had invented voice boxes for dogs. How did people in the olden days ever know when to let their dogs inside if their dogs couldn't talk? The Doggie Voice Box is such a wonderful invention. I'm so happy that I live in the year 2090!

What time of day is it? ___night___

What season is it? ___fall___

What year does this story take place? ___2090___

One Step Further
Brainstorm ideas for a story.
What is the setting of your story?

Second Grade Essentials

Tooth Tales

107

Directions: Answer the questions using information from the article about your teeth.

What are your teeth made of? ___enamel___
Highlight where you found the answer.

What is the hardest material in your body? ___enamel___
Highlight where you found the answer.

How many different types of teeth are in your mouth? ___four___
Highlight where you found the answer.

What are your four very pointy teeth called? ___canines___
Highlight where you found the answer.

How many teeth do adults have? ___32___
Highlight where you found the answer.

What teeth are used for biting? ___incisors___
Highlight where you found the answer.

How many molars do people have? ___12___
Highlight where you found the answer.

One Step Further
How many teeth do you have?
How many teeth have you lost?

Second Grade Essentials

Hermit Crabs

108

Directions: Read about hermit crabs. Use what you learn to finish the sentences.

The hermit crab lives in a shell in or near the ocean. It does not make its own shell. It moves into a shell left by another sea animal. As the hermit crab grows, it gets too big for its shell. It will hunt for a new shell. It will feel the new shell with its claw. If the shell feels just right, the crab will leave its old shell and move into the bigger one. It might even take a shell away from another hermit crab.

1. This story is mostly about the ___hermit crab___
2. The hermit crab lives ___in a shell___
3. When it gets too big for its shell, it will ___hunt for a new shell___
4. The crab will feel the shell with its ___claw___
5. It might take a shell away from ___another hermit crab___

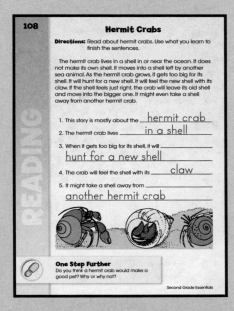

One Step Further
Do you think a hermit crab would make a good pet? Why or why not?

Second Grade Essentials

The Statue of Liberty

109

Directions: Read the facts below. Then, read each sentence below. If it is true, put a **T** on the line. If it is false, put an **F** on the line.

The Statue of Liberty is a symbol of the United States. It stands for freedom. It is the tallest statue in the United States.

The statue is of a woman wearing a robe. She is holding a torch in her right hand. She is holding a book in her left hand. She is wearing a crown. The Statue of Liberty was a gift from the country of France.

Each year, people come from all over the world to visit the statue. Not only do they look at it, they can also go inside the statue. At one time, visitors could go all the way up into the arm. In 1916, the arm was closed to visitors because it was too dangerous. The Statue of Liberty is located on an island in New York Harbor.

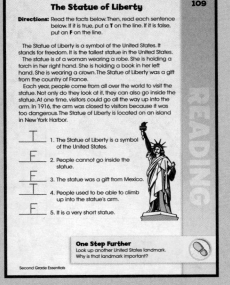

___T___ 1. The Statue of Liberty is a symbol of the United States.

___F___ 2. People cannot go inside the statue.

___F___ 3. The statue was a gift from Mexico.

___T___ 4. People used to be able to climb up into the statue's arm.

___F___ 5. It is a very short statue.

One Step Further
Look up another United States landmark.
Why is that landmark important?

Second Grade Essentials

Sticklebacks

110

Directions: Read about the stickleback fish. Use the article to help pick the correct answers to fill in the blanks. Circle the correct answer.

Sticklebacks are small fish. They have small spines along their backs. The spines keep other fish from trying to swallow them.

Stickleback fish are odd because the male builds the nest for the eggs. He makes the nest out of water plants and sticks. He makes it in the shape of a barrel and glues it together. He uses a thread-like material from his body to glue the nest together.

When the nest is ready, the mother fish comes. She lays her eggs and goes away. The father stays by the nest and guards the eggs. After the eggs hatch, he stays with the baby fish for a few days. If other sea animals try to eat the baby sticklebacks, he will fight them. He keeps the baby fish safe until they can care for themselves.

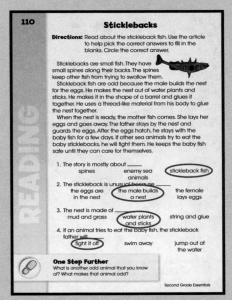

1. The story is mostly about _____
   spines | enemy sea animals | (stickleback fish)

2. The stickleback is unusual because
   the eggs are in the nest | (the male builds a nest) | the female lays eggs

3. The nest is made of
   mud and grass | (water plants and sticks) | string and glue

4. If an animal tries to eat the baby fish, the stickleback father will
   (fight it off) | swim away | jump out of the water

One Step Further
What is another odd animal that you know of? What makes that animal odd?

Second Grade Essentials

238

ANSWER KEY

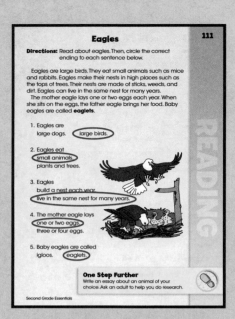

Eagles 111

Directions: Read about eagles. Then, circle the correct ending to each sentence below.

Eagles are large birds. They eat small animals such as mice and rabbits. Eagles make their nests in high places such as the tops of trees. Their nests are made of sticks, weeds, and dirt. Eagles can live in the same nest for many years.

The mother eagle lays one or two eggs each year. When she sits on the eggs, the father eagle brings her food. Baby eagles are called **eaglets**.

1. Eagles are
   large dogs.   (large birds.)

2. Eagles eat
   (small animals,)
   plants and trees.

3. Eagles
   build a nest each year.
   (live in the same nest for many years.)

4. The mother eagle lays
   (one or two eggs.)
   three or four eggs.

5. Baby eagles are called
   igloos.   (eaglets.)

READING

One Step Further
Write an essay about an animal of your choice. Ask an adult to help you do research.

Second Grade Essentials

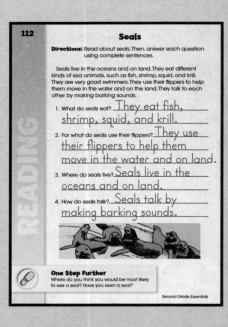

112 **Seals**

Directions: Read about seals. Then, answer each question using complete sentences.

Seals live in the oceans and on land. They eat different kinds of sea animals, such as fish, shrimp, squid, and krill. They are very good swimmers. They use their flippers to help them move in the water and on the land. They talk to each other by making barking sounds.

1. What do seals eat? They eat fish, shrimp, squid, and krill.

2. For what do seals use their flippers? They use their flippers to help them move in the water and on land.

3. Where do seals live? Seals live in the oceans and on land.

4. How do seals talk? Seals talk by making barking sounds.

READING

One Step Further
Where do you think you would be most likely to see a seal? Have you seen a seal?

Second Grade Essentials

114 **So Many Vegetables**

Directions: Count the number of each vegetable in the picture. Write the number in the correct box.

8   15   13   10
10   12   17

MATH

One Step Further
Name your favorite vegetable. Name your favorite fruit. Which do you like better?

Second Grade Essentials

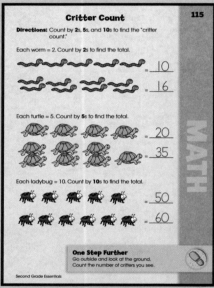

Critter Count 115

Directions: Count by **2**s, **5**s, and **10**s to find the "critter count."

Each worm = 2. Count by **2**s to find the total.

= 10
= 16

Each turtle = 5. Count by **5**s to find the total.

= 20
= 35

Each ladybug = 10. Count by **10**s to find the total.

= 50
= 60

MATH

One Step Further
Go outside and look at the ground. Count the number of critters you see.

Second Grade Essentials

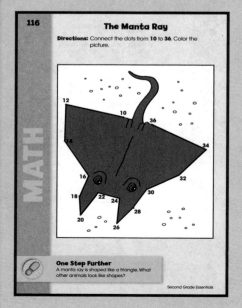

116 **The Manta Ray**

Directions: Connect the dots from **10** to **36**. Color the picture.

MATH

One Step Further
A manta ray is shaped like a triangle. What other animals look like shapes?

Second Grade Essentials

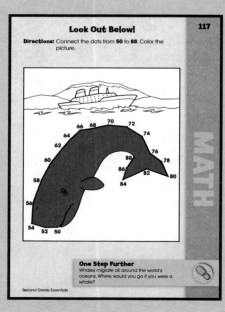

Look Out Below! 117

Directions: Connect the dots from **50** to **88**. Color the picture.

MATH

One Step Further
Whales migrate all around the world's oceans. Where would you go if you were a whale?

Second Grade Essentials

Second Grade Essentials

118

Sharpy Swordfish

Directions: Connect the dots from **3** to **27**. Color the picture.

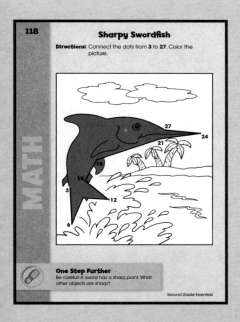

MATH

One Step Further
Be careful! A sword has a sharp point. What other objects are sharp?

Second Grade Essentials

119

What Shark Is This?

Directions: Connect the dots from **24** to **72**. Color the picture.

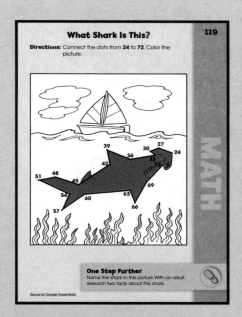

MATH

One Step Further
Name the shark in this picture. With an adult, research two facts about this shark.

Second Grade Essentials

120

Is It a Bird?

Directions: Connect the dots from **0** to **24**. Color the picture.

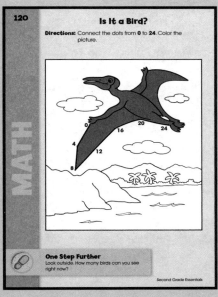

MATH

One Step Further
Look outside. How many birds can you see right now?

Second Grade Essentials

121

A Crest for a Head

Directions: Connect the dots from **8** to **40**. Color the picture.

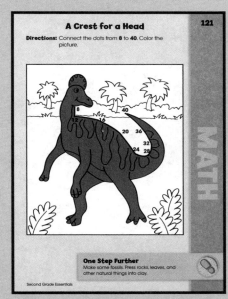

MATH

One Step Further
Make some fossils. Press rocks, leaves, and other natural things into clay.

Second Grade Essentials

122

Rapunzel

Directions: Connect the dots from **5** to **70**. Color the picture.

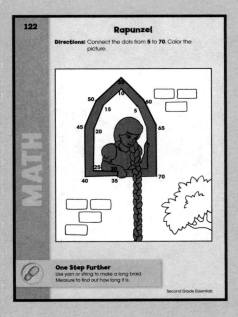

MATH

One Step Further
Use yarn or string to make a long braid. Measure to find out how long it is.

Second Grade Essentials

123

The Princess & the Pea

Directions: Connect the dots from **5** to **100**. Color the picture.

MATH

One Step Further
Change one thing in a room. Can a friend tell what change you made?

Second Grade Essentials

Second Grade Essentials

124 — Largest and Smallest

Directions: In each shape, circle the smallest number. Draw a square around the largest number.

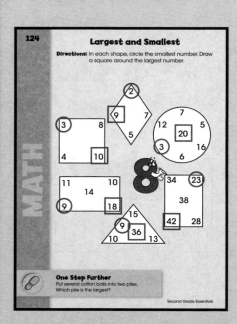

One Step Further
Put several cotton balls into two piles. Which pile is the largest?

Second Grade Essentials

125 — Fishing for Answers

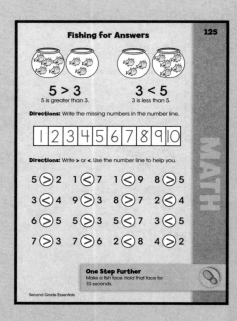

$5 > 3$
5 is greater than 3.

$3 < 5$
3 is less than 5.

Directions: Write the missing numbers in the number line.

| 1 | 2 | 3 | 4 | 5 | 6 | 7 | 8 | 9 | 10 |

Directions: Write > or <. Use the number line to help you.

$5 > 2$ $1 < 7$ $1 < 9$ $8 > 5$

$3 < 4$ $9 > 3$ $8 > 7$ $2 < 4$

$6 > 5$ $5 > 3$ $5 < 7$ $3 < 5$

$7 > 3$ $7 > 6$ $2 < 8$ $4 > 2$

One Step Further
Make a fish face. Hold that face for 10 seconds.

Second Grade Essentials

126 — Who Has the Most?

Directions: Circle the correct answer.

1. Traci has 3 🐛s.
   Bob has 4 🐛s.
   Bill has 5 🐛s.
   Who has the most 🐛s?
   Traci   Bob   **(Bill)**

2. Pam has 7 🐞s.
   Joe has 5 🐞s.
   Jane has 6 🐞s.
   Who has the most 🐞s?
   (Pam)   Joe   Jane

3. Jennifer has 23 🐝s.
   Sandy has 19 🐝s.
   Jack has 25 🐝s.
   Who has the most 🐝s?
   Jennifer   Sandy   **(Jack)**

4. Ali has 19 🐛s.
   Burt has 18 🐛s.
   Brent has 17 🐛s.
   Who has the most 🐛s?
   (Ali)   Burt   Brent

5. The boys have 14 🐞s.
   The girls have 16 🐞s.
   The teachers have 17 🐞s.
   Who has the most 🐞s?
   boys   girls   **(teachers)**

6. Rose has 12 🐛s.
   Betsy has 11 🐛s.
   Leslie has 13 🐛s.
   Who has the most 🐛s?
   Rose   Betsy   **(Leslie)**

One Step Further
Get with a friend and count all your teddy bears. Who has the most?

Second Grade Essentials

127 — Who Has the Fewest?

Directions: Circle the correct answer.

1. Pat had 4 🐞s.
   Charles had 3 🐞s.
   Andrea had 5 🐞s.
   Who had the fewest number of 🐞s?
   Pat   **(Charles)**   Andrea

2. Jeff has 5 🐞s.
   John has 4 🐞s.
   Bill has 6 🐞s.
   Who has the fewest number of 🐞s?
   Jeff   **(John)**   Bill

3. Jane has 7 ○s.
   Susan has 9 ○s.
   Fred has 8 ○s.
   Who has the fewest number of ○s?
   (Jane)   Susan   Fred

4. Charles bought 12 ○s.
   Rose bought 6 ○s.
   Dawn bought 24 ○s.
   Who bought the fewest number of ○?
   Charles   **(Rose)**   Dawn

5. John had 9 🫘s.
   Jack had 8 🫘s.
   Mark had 7 🫘s.
   Who had the fewest number of 🫘s?
   John   Jack   **(Mark)**

6. Edith bought 12 ⊝s.
   Michelle bought 16 ⊝s.
   Marty bought 13 ⊝s.
   Who bought the fewest number of ⊝s?
   (Edith)   Michelle   Marty

One Step Further
Count the lamps in each room of your home. Which room has the fewest?

Second Grade Essentials

128 — Signs of Gain

Directions: Roll a die. Write the number from the die in the top box. Add to find the sum. Roll again to make each sentence different.

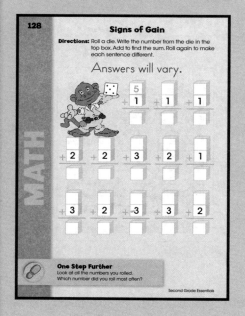

Answers will vary.

One Step Further
Look at all the numbers you rolled. Which number did you roll most often?

Second Grade Essentials

129 — Counting Up

Directions: Count up to get the sum. Write the missing number in each blank.

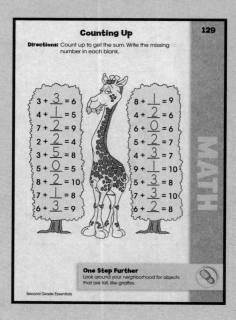

$3 + 3 = 6$
$4 + 1 = 5$
$7 + 2 = 9$
$2 + 2 = 4$
$3 + 5 = 8$
$5 + 0 = 5$
$8 + 2 = 10$
$7 + 1 = 8$
$6 + 3 = 9$

$8 + 1 = 9$
$4 + 2 = 6$
$6 + 0 = 6$
$5 + 2 = 7$
$4 + 3 = 7$
$9 + 1 = 10$
$5 + 3 = 8$
$7 + 3 = 10$
$6 + 2 = 8$

One Step Further
Look around your neighborhood for objects that are tall, like giraffes.

Second Grade Essentials

ANSWER KEY

130 — Snorkeling Solutions

Directions: Add the numbers in each mask. Write the sums in the bubbles. Color the bubbles of the four largest sums.

- 11 — 5+6
- 17 — 9+8
- 6 — 5+1
- 16 — 9+7
- 14 — 8+6
- 14 — 7+7
- 18 — 9+9
- 11 — 2+9
- 20 — 10+10
- 14 — 9+5
- 15 — 6+9
- 13 — 7+6

One Step Further
How long can you hold your breath? Ask an adult to time you.

Second Grade Essentials

131 — Add the Apples

Directions: Match the addition sentences with their sums.

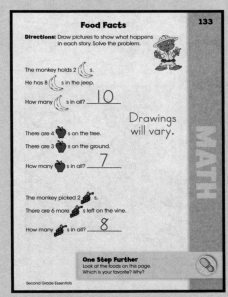

- 3 + 2 = 10
- 6 + 8 = 14
- 5 + 5 = 5
- 8 + 2 = 15
- 9 + 4 = 4
- 2 + 2 = 10
- 1 + 2 = 11
- 6 + 7 = 3
- 5 + 6 = 13
- 6 + 6 = 12
- 6 + 3 = 9
- 3 + 4 = 7
- 6 + 2 = 8
- 1 + 1 = 6
- 1 + 5 = 2
- 7 + 2 = 15
- 6 + 9 = 9
- 12 + 1 = 13
- 10 + 1 = 14
- 9 + 5 = 8
- 7 + 1 = 11

One Step Further
How many apples did you eat this week? Try to eat more apples next week.

Second Grade Essentials

132 — Problem Solving

Directions: Solve each problem.

Example:

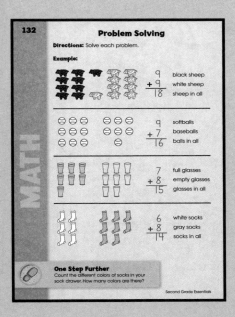

9	black sheep
+ 9	white sheep
18	sheep in all

9	softballs
+ 7	baseballs
16	balls in all

7	full glasses
+ 8	empty glasses
15	glasses in all

6	white socks
+ 8	gray socks
14	socks in all

One Step Further
Count the different colors of socks in your sock drawer. How many colors are there?

Second Grade Essentials

133 — Food Facts

Directions: Draw pictures to show what happens in each story. Solve the problem.

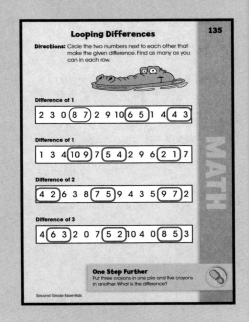

The monkey holds 2 🍌 s.
He has 8 🍌 s in the jeep.
How many 🍌 s in all? **10**

Drawings will vary.

There are 4 🍎 s on the tree.
There are 3 🍎 s on the ground.
How many 🍎 s in all? **7**

The monkey picked 2 🍇 s.
There are 6 more 🍇 s left on the vine.
How many 🍇 s in all? **8**

One Step Further
Look at the foods on this page. Which is your favorite? Why?

Second Grade Essentials

134 — Leaves Leaving the Limb

Directions: Subtract to find the difference. Use the code to color the leaves.

Code: 0 = green   1 = red   2 = ___   3 = brown

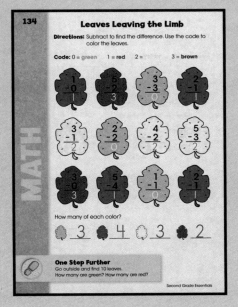

How many of each color?
🍃 **3**   🍂 **4**   🍃 **3**   🍂 **2**

One Step Further
Go outside and find 10 leaves. How many are green? How many are red?

Second Grade Essentials

135 — Looping Differences

Directions: Circle the two numbers next to each other that make the given difference. Find as many as you can in each row.

Difference of 1
2 3 0 (8 7) 2 9 10 (6 5) 1 4 (4 3)

Difference of 1
1 3 4 (10 9) (7 5) 4 2 9 6 (2 1) 7

Difference of 2
4 2 6 3 8 (7 5) 9 4 3 5 (9 7) 2

Difference of 3
4 (6 3) 2 0 7 (5 2) 10 4 0 (8 5) 3

One Step Further
Put three crayons in one pile and five crayons in another. What is the difference?

Second Grade Essentials

Second Grade Essentials

ANSWER KEY

MATH

136

Subtraction Facts

Directions: Subtract.

Example:

$13 - 5 = 8$ $14 - 9 = 5$

$14 - 8 = 6$ $13 - 4 = 9$

Directions: Subtract.

12 − 7 = 5	10 − 2 = 8	13 − 4 = 9	14 − 9 = 5	11 − 8 = 3	14 − 5 = 9
14 − 6 = 8	12 − 8 = 4	13 − 5 = 8	10 − 6 = 4	13 − 6 = 7	13 − 7 = 6
11 − 6 = 5	13 − 9 = 4	14 − 4 = 0	12 − 3 = 9	14 − 7 = 7	13 − 8 = 5

One Step Further
Count the basketballs in your school.
Count the soccer balls.

Second Grade Essentials

137

Subtraction Facts

Directions: Subtract.

Example:

$15 - 7 = 8$ $16 - 9 = 7$

$17 - 8 = 9$ $18 - 9 = 9$

Directions: Subtract.

18 − 9 = 9	13 − 5 = 8	16 − 8 = 8	17 − 9 = 8	14 − 6 = 8	13 − 9 = 4
17 − 8 = 9	15 − 9 = 6	14 − 5 = 9	13 − 6 = 7	16 − 7 = 9	12 − 4 = 8
14 − 7 = 7	15 − 8 = 7	16 − 9 = 7	12 − 7 = 5	15 − 7 = 8	13 − 4 = 9

One Step Further
How many pencils can you find in your desk at school?

Second Grade Essentials

138

"Grrreat" Picture

Directions: Subtract. Write the answer in the space. Then, color the spaces according to the answers.

1 = white   4 = green   7 = pink   10 = red
2 = purple   5 =   8 = gray
3 = black   6 = blue   9 = orange

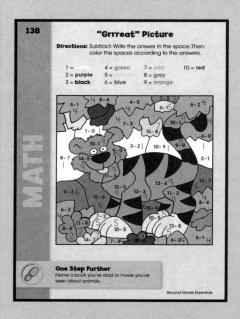

One Step Further
Name a book you've read or movie you've seen about animals.

Second Grade Essentials

139

Swamp Stories

Directions: Read the story. Subtract to find the difference. Write the number in the box.

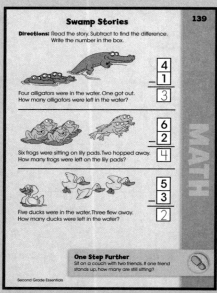

Four alligators were in the water. One got out. How many alligators were left in the water?

$4 - 1 = 3$

Six frogs were sitting on lily pads. Two hopped away. How many frogs were left on the lily pads?

$6 - 2 = 4$

Five ducks were in the water. Three flew away. How many ducks were left in the water?

$5 - 3 = 2$

One Step Further
Sit on a couch with two friends. If one friend stands up, how many are still sitting?

Second Grade Essentials

140

Two-Digit Addition

Directions: Study the example. Follow the steps to add.

Example:
$$33 + 41$$

Step 1: Add the ones.   **Step 2:** Add the tens.

tens	ones
3	3
+4	1
	4

tens	ones
3	3
+4	1
7	4

tens	ones
4	2
+2	4
6	6

tens	ones
5	0
+4	7
9	7

24 + 62 = 86	15 + 23 = 38	38 + 61 = 99	11 + 26 = 37	37 + 42 = 79	72 + 11 = 83
25 + 42 = 67	62 + 14 = 76	32 + 44 = 76	25 + 13 = 38	82 + 6 = 88	91 + 5 = 96

One Step Further
Ask two adults how old they are. Add their ages together.

Second Grade Essentials

141

Picture This

Directions: Add the ones, then the tens in each problem. Then, write the sum in the blank.

Example:
2 tens and 6 ones
+ 1 ten and 3 ones
3 tens and 9 ones = 39

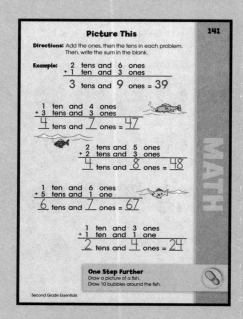

1 ten and 4 ones
+ 3 tens and 3 ones
4 tens and 7 ones = 47

2 tens and 5 ones
+ 2 tens and 3 ones
4 tens and 8 ones = 48

1 ten and 6 ones
+ 5 tens and 1 one
6 tens and 7 ones = 67

1 ten and 3 ones
+ 1 ten and 1 one
2 tens and 4 ones = 24

One Step Further
Draw a picture of a fish. Draw 10 bubbles around the fish.

Second Grade Essentials

MATH

142 Two-Digit Addition: Regrouping

Addition is "putting together" or adding two or more numbers to find the sum. Regrouping is using **ten ones** to form **one ten**, **ten tens** to form **one 100**, **fifteen ones** to form **one ten** and **five ones**, and so on.

Directions: Study the examples. Follow the steps to add.

Example:
```
  14
+  8
```

Step 1: Add the ones.
Step 2: Regroup the tens.
Step 3: Add the tens.

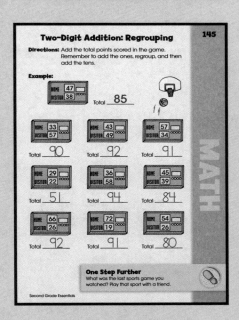

28 +17 = 45	32 +38 = 70	54 +25 = 79
19 +55 = 74	44 +48 = 92	25 +64 = 89

One Step Further
Draw circles for 20 seconds. Then, draw circles for 10 seconds. How many circles did you draw?

Second Grade Essentials

143 Two-Digit Addition

Directions:
Add the ones. Rename 11 as 10 + 1. Add the tens.
```
  38      8         38       38
+43    + 3       +43      +43
       11 or 10 + 1        81
```

Directions: Add.

Example:

17 +34 = 51	26 +47 = 73	47 +35 = 82	68 +24 = 92	37 +28 = 65
29 +48 = 77	58 +27 = 85	69 +17 = 86	78 +13 = 91	19 +44 = 63
55 +28 = 83	27 +35 = 62	39 +52 = 91	57 +27 = 84	38 +36 = 74
49 +43 = 92	65 +18 = 83	23 +18 = 41	64 +18 = 82	46 +39 = 85

One Step Further
How many states are there? Add that number to your age. What is the total?

Second Grade Essentials

144 Two-Digit Addition

Directions: Add the total points scored in each game. Remember to add **ones** first and **tens** second.

Example:
HOME 22 / VISITOR 17   Total 39

HOME 28 / VISITOR 30 Total 58	HOME 55 / VISITOR 21 Total 76	HOME 14 / VISITOR 33 Total 47
HOME 24 / VISITOR 13 Total 37	HOME 46 / VISITOR 32 Total 78	HOME 83 / VISITOR 06 Total 89
HOME 30 / VISITOR 20 Total 50	HOME 17 / VISITOR 42 Total 59	HOME 24 / VISITOR 45 Total 69

One Step Further
What was the score of your favorite team's last game? Add the numbers together.

Second Grade Essentials

145 Two-Digit Addition: Regrouping

Directions: Add the total points scored in the game. Remember to add the ones, regroup, and then add the tens.

Example:
HOME 47 / VISITOR 38   Total 85

HOME 33 / VISITOR 57 Total 90	HOME 43 / VISITOR 49 Total 92	HOME 57 / VISITOR 34 Total 91
HOME 29 / VISITOR 22 Total 51	HOME 36 / VISITOR 58 Total 94	HOME 45 / VISITOR 39 Total 84
HOME 66 / VISITOR 26 Total 92	HOME 72 / VISITOR 19 Total 91	HOME 54 / VISITOR 26 Total 80

One Step Further
What was the last sports game you watched? Play that sport with a friend.

Second Grade Essentials

146 Problem Solving

Directions: Solve each problem.

Example:

There are 20 men in the plane.
Then, 30 women get in the plane.
How many men and women are in the plane?
```
  20
+ 30
  50
```

Jill buys 10 apples.
Carol buys 20 apples.
How many apples in all?
```
  10
+ 20
  30
```

There are 30 ears of corn in one pile.
There are 50 ears of corn in another pile.
How many ears of corn in all?
```
  30
+ 50
  80
```

Henry cut 40 pieces of wood.
Art cut 20 pieces of wood.
How many pieces of wood were cut?
```
  40
+ 20
  60
```

One Step Further
Name something you collect.
How many items are there in your collection?

Second Grade Essentials

147 Problem Solving

Directions: Solve each problem.

Example:

16 boys ride their bikes to school.
18 girls ride their bikes to school.
How many bikes are ridden to school?
```
  16
+ 18
  34
```

Dad reads 26 pages.
Mike reads 37 pages.
How many pages did Dad and Mike read?
```
  26
+ 37
  63
```

Tiffany counts 46 stars.
Mike counts 39 stars.
How many stars did they count?
```
  46
+ 39
  85
```

Mom has 29 golf balls.
Dad has 43 golf balls.
How many golf balls do they have?
```
  29
+ 43
  72
```

One Step Further
What is your favorite book?
How many pages is it?

Second Grade Essentials

MATH

148 — Two-Digit Subtraction

Directions: Look at the example. Follow the steps to subtract.

Example:
$$28 - 14$$

Step 1: Subtract the ones.
tens	ones
2	8
-1	4
	4

Step 2: Subtract the tens.
tens	ones
2	8
-1	4
1	4

24	61	77	85	57	87
-12	-30	-44	-24	-23	-33
12	31	33	61	34	54

84	98	74	58	82	98
-30	-16	-32	-38	-40	-36
54	82	42	20	42	62

One Step Further
Ask an adult to write more subtraction problems. How fast can you solve them?

Second Grade Essentials

149 — All Aboard

Directions: Count the tens and ones and write the numbers. Then, subtract to solve the problems.

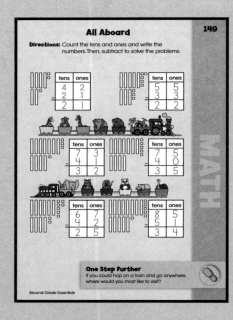

tens	ones
4	2
2	1
2	1

tens	ones
5	5
3	3
2	2

tens	ones
7	3
4	1
3	2

tens	ones
7	5
5	0
2	5

tens	ones
6	7
4	2
2	5

tens	ones
8	5
5	1
3	4

One Step Further
If you could hop on a train and go anywhere, where would you most like to visit?

Second Grade Essentials

150 — Cookie Craze!

Directions: Subtract to solve the problems. Circle the answers. Color the cookies with answers greater than 30.

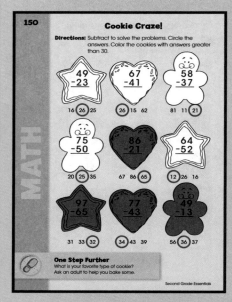

$49 - 23$ → 16 (26) 25
$67 - 41$ → (26) 15 62
$58 - 37$ → 81 11 (21)
$75 - 50$ → 20 (25) 35
$86 - 21$ → 67 86 (65)
$64 - 52$ → (12) 26 16
$97 - 65$ → 31 33 (32)
$77 - 43$ → (34) 43 39
$49 - 13$ → 56 (36) 37

One Step Further
What is your favorite type of cookie? Ask an adult to help you bake some.

Second Grade Essentials

151 — Prehistoric Problems

Directions: Solve the subtraction problems. Use the code to color the picture.

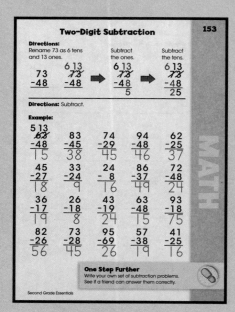

Code: 25 = blue   57 = green
31 = yellow   14 = orange
21 = brown   11 = red

$52 - 21 = 31$
$47 - 22 = 25$
$25 - 11 = 14$
$62 - 31 = 31$
$77 - 20 = 57$
$51 - 40 = 11$
$69 - 12 = 57$
$98 - 41 = 57$

One Step Further
Where might you see dinosaurs today? Write everything you know about dinosaurs.

Second Grade Essentials

152 — Two-Digit Subtraction: Regrouping

Subtraction is "taking away" or subtracting one number from another to find the difference. Regrouping is using **one ten** to form **ten ones**, **one 100** to form **ten tens**, and so on.

Directions: Study the examples. Follow the steps to subtract.

Example:
$$37 - 19$$

Step 1: Regroup.
Step 2: Subtract the ones.
Step 3: Subtract the tens.

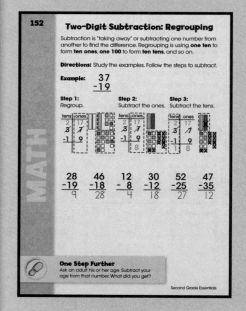

28	46	12	30	52	47
-19	-18	-8	-12	-25	-35
9	28	4	18	27	12

One Step Further
Ask an adult his or her age. Subtract your age from that number. What did you get?

Second Grade Essentials

153 — Two-Digit Subtraction

Directions: Rename 73 as 6 tens and 13 ones.

$$73 - 48 \quad → \quad \overset{6\ 13}{73} - 48 \quad → \quad \overset{6\ 13}{73} - 48 = 5 \quad → \quad \overset{6\ 13}{73} - 48 = 25$$

(Subtract the ones.) (Subtract the tens.)

Directions: Subtract.

Example:
$$\overset{5\ 13}{63} - 48 = 15$$

83	74	94	62
-45	-29	-48	-25
38	45	46	37

45	33	24	86	72
-27	-24	-8	-37	-48
18	9	16	49	24

36	26	43	63	93
-17	-18	-19	-48	-18
19	8	24	15	75

82	73	95	57	41
-26	-28	-69	-38	-25
56	45	26	19	16

One Step Further
Write your own set of subtraction problems. See if a friend can answer them correctly.

Second Grade Essentials

ANSWER KEY

154 — Subtraction With Regrouping

Directions: Subtract to find the difference. Regroup as needed. Color the spaces with differences of:

10–19 = red   50–59 = brown   30–39 = green
40–49 = _____   20–29 = blue   60–69 = orange

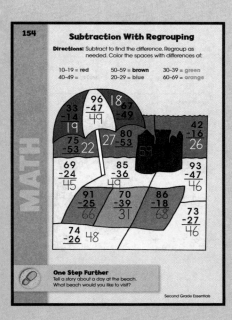

$96 - 47 = 49$
$33 - 14 = 19$
$67 - 49 = 18$
$42 - 16 = 26$
$75 - 53 = 22$
$80 - 53 = 27$
$69 - 24 = 45$
$85 - 36 = 49$
$93 - 47 = 46$
$91 - 25 = 66$
$70 - 39 = 31$
$86 - 18 = 68$
$73 - 27 = 46$
$74 - 26 = 48$

One Step Further
Tell a story about a day at the beach. What beach would you like to visit?

Second Grade Essentials

155 — Go "Fore" It!

Directions: Add or subtract using regrouping.

tens	ones
2	15
3	5
-2	7
	8

$56 - 27 = 29$
$40 - 16 = 24$
$35 + 27 = 62$
$42 - 14 = 28$
$44 + 28 = 72$
$93 - 39 = 54$
$97 - 48 = 49$
$73 - 24 = 49$
$33 + 18 = 51$
$56 - 17 = 39$
$68 - 49 = 19$
$77 - 68 = 9$
$49 + 32 = 81$
$27 + 19 = 46$

One Step Further
Go to a driving range with a friend. See who can hit a golf ball the farthest.

Second Grade Essentials

156 — Monster Math

Directions: Add or subtract using regrouping.

$84 - 56 = 28$
$36 - 19 = 17$
$41 - 17 = 24$
$65 - 28 = 37$
$52 - 28 = 24$
$72 - 19 = 53$
$48 - 30 = 18$
$84 - 27 = 57$
$33 - 15 = 18$
$33 + 18 = 51$
$57 - 39 = 18$
$64 + 17 = 81$
$25 + 35 = 60$

One Step Further
Make up a scary story about monsters. Tell it to a friend around a campfire.

Second Grade Essentials

157 — Problem Solving

Directions: Solve each problem.

Example:

Dad cooks 23 potatoes.
He uses 19 potatoes in the potato salad.
How many potatoes are left?
$23 - 19 = 4$

Susan draws 32 butterflies.
She colors 15 of them brown.
How many butterflies does she have left to color?
$32 - 15 = 17$

A book has 66 pages.
Pedro reads 39 pages.
How many pages are left to read?
$66 - 39 = 27$

Jerry picks up 34 seashells.
He puts 15 of them in a box.
How many does he have left?
$34 - 15 = 19$

One Step Further
Draw 14 circles. Color eight red and the rest blue. How many circles are blue?

Second Grade Essentials

158 — Adding Hundreds

5 hundreds	500	4 hundreds	400
+ 3 hundreds	+ 300	+ 5 hundreds	+ 500
8 hundreds	800	9 hundreds	900

Directions: Add.

3 hundreds + 1 hundred = 4 hundreds; $300 + 100 = 400$
6 hundreds + 2 hundreds = 8 hundreds; $600 + 200 = 800$
$200 + 200 = 400$
$100 + 700 = 800$
$600 + 300 = 900$
$400 + 500 = 900$
$300 + 400 = 700$
$800 + 100 = 900$
$400 + 400 = 800$
$700 + 200 = 900$
$500 + 100 = 600$
$100 + 600 = 700$
$500 + 200 = 700$
$300 + 200 = 500$
$300 + 300 = 600$
$400 + 200 = 600$
$300 + 500 = 800$
$200 + 100 = 300$

One Step Further
How old would you be in 100 years and in 300 years? Add those numbers together.

Second Grade Essentials

159 — Subtracting Hundreds

8 hundreds	800	6 hundreds	600
- 3 hundreds	- 300	- 2 hundreds	- 200
5 hundreds	500	4 hundreds	400

Directions: Subtract.

9 hundreds - 7 hundreds = 2 hundreds; $900 - 700 = 200$
3 hundreds - 1 hundred = 2 hundreds; $300 - 100 = 200$
$700 - 300 = 400$
$500 - 400 = 100$
$900 - 400 = 500$
$800 - 500 = 300$
$600 - 500 = 100$
$300 - 200 = 100$
$500 - 100 = 400$
$400 - 200 = 200$
$900 - 100 = 800$
$800 - 400 = 400$
$600 - 200 = 400$
$500 - 300 = 200$

One Step Further
Pretend you have $700. If you buy a toy that costs $100, how much will you have left?

Second Grade Essentials

Second Grade Essentials

160 — Three-Digit Addition

$$\begin{array}{r}245\\+253\\\hline 8\end{array}\ \Rightarrow\ \begin{array}{r}245\\+253\\\hline 98\end{array}\ \Rightarrow\ \begin{array}{r}245\\+253\\\hline 498\end{array}$$

Directions: Add.

Examples:

$$\begin{array}{r}745\\+\ 23\\\hline 768\end{array}\qquad\begin{array}{r}623\\+156\\\hline 779\end{array}$$

Add the ones.
Add the tens.
Add the hundreds.

$$\begin{array}{r}415\\+342\\\hline 757\end{array}\quad\begin{array}{r}566\\+\ 33\\\hline 599\end{array}\quad\begin{array}{r}373\\+221\\\hline 594\end{array}\quad\begin{array}{r}160\\+334\\\hline 494\end{array}$$

$$\begin{array}{r}835\\+\ 42\\\hline 877\end{array}\quad\begin{array}{r}642\\+251\\\hline 893\end{array}\quad\begin{array}{r}287\\+412\\\hline 699\end{array}\quad\begin{array}{r}723\\+\ 45\\\hline 768\end{array}$$

$$\begin{array}{r}133\\+522\\\hline 655\end{array}\quad\begin{array}{r}454\\+324\\\hline 778\end{array}\quad\begin{array}{r}314\\+602\\\hline 916\end{array}\quad\begin{array}{r}654\\+235\\\hline 889\end{array}$$

One Step Further
Choose two random three-digit numbers.
Add them together.

Second Grade Essentials

161 — Three-Digit Subtraction

Directions:
Subtract the ones. / Subtract the tens. / Subtract the hundreds.

$$\begin{array}{r}746\\-424\\\hline 2\end{array}\ \Rightarrow\ \begin{array}{r}746\\-424\\\hline 22\end{array}\ \Rightarrow\ \begin{array}{r}746\\-424\\\hline 322\end{array}$$

Directions: Subtract.

Examples:

$$\begin{array}{r}879\\-\ 46\\\hline 833\end{array}\qquad\begin{array}{r}586\\-142\\\hline 444\end{array}$$

Subtract the ones.
Subtract the tens.
Subtract the hundreds.

$$\begin{array}{r}635\\-423\\\hline 212\end{array}\quad\begin{array}{r}478\\-241\\\hline 237\end{array}\quad\begin{array}{r}338\\-\ 27\\\hline 311\end{array}\quad\begin{array}{r}957\\-734\\\hline 223\end{array}$$

$$\begin{array}{r}297\\-145\\\hline 152\end{array}\quad\begin{array}{r}846\\-325\\\hline 521\end{array}\quad\begin{array}{r}769\\-514\\\hline 255\end{array}\quad\begin{array}{r}653\\-142\\\hline 511\end{array}$$

One Step Further
Choose two random three-digit numbers.
Subtract the smaller one from the bigger one.

Second Grade Essentials

162 — Problem Solving

Directions: Solve each problem.

Example:

Ria packed 300 boxes.
Melvin packed 200 boxes.
How many boxes did Ria and Melvin pack?
$$\begin{array}{r}200\\+300\\\hline 500\end{array}$$

Santo typed 500 letters.
Hale typed 400 letters.
How many letters did they type?
$$\begin{array}{r}500\\+400\\\hline 900\end{array}$$

Paula used 100 paper clips.
Milton used 600 paper clips.
How many paper clips did they use?
$$\begin{array}{r}100\\+600\\\hline 700\end{array}$$

The grocery store sold 400 red apples.
The grocery store also sold 100 yellow apples.
How many apples did the grocery store sell in all?
$$\begin{array}{r}400\\+100\\\hline 500\end{array}$$

One Step Further
Go to the grocery store with an adult. Guess
how many apples are being sold.

Second Grade Essentials

163 — Problem Solving

Directions: Solve each problem.

Example:

Gene collected 342 rocks.
Lester collected 201 rocks.
How many rocks did they collect?
$$\begin{array}{r}342\\+201\\\hline 543\end{array}$$

Tina jumped the rope 403 times.
Henry jumped the rope 426 times.
How many times did they jump?
$$\begin{array}{r}403\\+426\\\hline 829\end{array}$$

There are 210 people wearing blue hats.
There are 432 people wearing red hats.
How many hats in all?
$$\begin{array}{r}210\\+432\\\hline 642\end{array}$$

Asta used 135 paper plates.
Clyde used 143 paper plates.
How many paper plates did they use in all?
$$\begin{array}{r}135\\+143\\\hline 278\end{array}$$

One Step Further
Go outside and collect rocks. How many did
you find?

Second Grade Essentials

164 — Problem Solving

Directions: Solve each problem.

There are 236 boys in school.
There are 250 girls in school.
How many boys and girls are in school?
$$\begin{array}{r}236\\+250\\\hline 486\end{array}$$

Mary saw 131 cars.
Marvin saw 268 trucks.
How many cars and trucks did they see in all?
$$\begin{array}{r}131\\+268\\\hline 399\end{array}$$

Jack has 427 pennies.
Jill has 370 pennies.
How many pennies do they have in all?
$$\begin{array}{r}427\\+370\\\hline 797\end{array}$$

There are 582 red apples.
There are 206 yellow apples.
How many apples are there in all?
$$\begin{array}{r}582\\+206\\\hline 788\end{array}$$

One Step Further
Look in the parking lot of your school. Count
the cars and trucks. Add them together.

Second Grade Essentials

165 — Problem Solving

Directions: Solve each problem.

Example:

The grocery store buys 568 cans of beans.
It sells 345 cans of beans.
How many cans of beans are left?
$$\begin{array}{r}568\\-345\\\hline 223\end{array}$$

The cooler holds 732 gallons of milk.
It has 412 gallons of milk in it.
How many more gallons of milk
will it take to fill the cooler?
$$\begin{array}{r}732\\-412\\\hline 320\end{array}$$

Ann does 635 push-ups.
Carl does 421 push-ups.
How many more push-ups does Ann do?
$$\begin{array}{r}635\\-421\\\hline 214\end{array}$$

Kurt has 386 pennies.
Neal has 32 pennies.
How many more pennies does Kurt have?
$$\begin{array}{r}386\\-\ 32\\\hline 354\end{array}$$

One Step Further
How many push-ups can you do? Practice
every day until you can double your total.

Second Grade Essentials

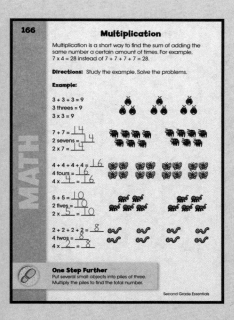

166 Multiplication

Multiplication is a short way to find the sum of adding the same number a certain amount of times. For example, 7 x 4 = 28 instead of 7 + 7 + 7 + 7 = 28.

Directions: Study the example. Solve the problems.

Example:

3 + 3 + 3 = 9
3 threes = 9
3 x 3 = 9

7 + 7 = 14
2 sevens = 14
2 x 7 = 14

4 + 4 + 4 + 4 = 16
4 fours = 16
4 x 4 = 16

5 + 5 = 10
2 fives = 10
2 x 5 = 10

2 + 2 + 2 + 2 = 8
4 twos = 8
4 x 2 = 8

One Step Further
Put several small objects into piles of three. Multiply the piles to find the total number.

Second Grade Essentials

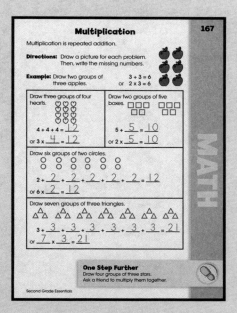

167 Multiplication

Multiplication is repeated addition.

Directions: Draw a picture for each problem. Then, write the missing numbers.

Example: Draw two groups of three apples.
3 + 3 = 6
or 2 x 3 = 6

Draw three groups of four hearts.
4 + 4 + 4 = 12
or 3 x 4 = 12

Draw two groups of five boxes.
5 + 5 = 10
or 2 x 5 = 10

Draw six groups of two circles.
2 + 2 + 2 + 2 + 2 + 2 = 12
or 6 x 2 = 12

Draw seven groups of three triangles.
3 + 3 + 3 + 3 + 3 + 3 + 3 = 21
or 7 x 3 = 21

One Step Further
Draw four groups of three stars. Ask a friend to multiply them together.

Second Grade Essentials

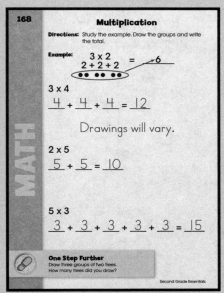

168 Multiplication

Directions: Study the example. Draw the groups and write the total.

Example:
3 x 2
2 + 2 + 2 = 6

3 x 4
4 + 4 + 4 = 12

Drawings will vary.

2 x 5
5 + 5 = 10

5 x 3
3 + 3 + 3 + 3 + 3 = 15

One Step Further
Draw three groups of two trees. How many trees did you draw?

Second Grade Essentials

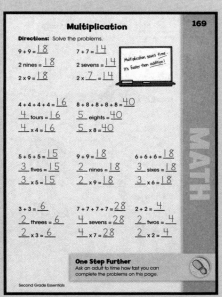

169 Multiplication

Directions: Solve the problems.

9 + 9 = 18
2 nines = 18
2 x 9 = 18

7 + 7 = 14
2 sevens = 14
2 x 7 = 14

Multiplication saves time. It's faster than addition!

4 + 4 + 4 + 4 = 16
4 fours = 16
4 x 4 = 16

8 + 8 + 8 + 8 + 8 = 40
5 eights = 40
5 x 8 = 40

5 + 5 + 5 = 15
3 fives = 15
3 x 5 = 15

9 + 9 = 18
2 nines = 18
2 x 9 = 18

6 + 6 + 6 = 18
3 sixes = 18
3 x 6 = 18

3 + 3 = 6
2 threes = 6
2 x 3 = 6

7 + 7 + 7 + 7 = 28
4 sevens = 28
4 x 7 = 28

2 + 2 = 4
2 twos = 4
2 x 2 = 4

One Step Further
Ask an adult to time how fast you can complete the problems on this page.

Second Grade Essentials

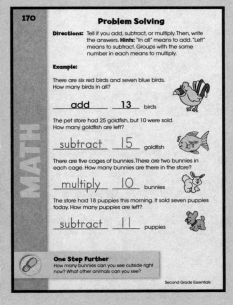

170 Problem Solving

Directions: Tell if you add, subtract, or multiply. Then, write the answers. **Hints:** "In all" means to add. "Left" means to subtract. Groups with the same number in each means to multiply.

Example:

There are six red birds and seven blue birds. How many birds in all?
add 13 birds

The pet store had 25 goldfish, but 10 were sold. How many goldfish are left?
subtract 15 goldfish

There are five cages of bunnies. There are two bunnies in each cage. How many bunnies are there in the store?
multiply 10 bunnies

The store had 18 puppies this morning. It sold seven puppies today. How many puppies are left?
subtract 11 puppies

One Step Further
How many bunnies can you see outside right now? What other animals can you see?

Second Grade Essentials

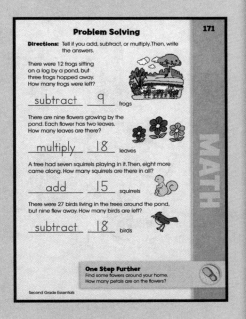

171 Problem Solving

Directions: Tell if you add, subtract, or multiply. Then, write the answers.

There were 12 frogs sitting on a log by a pond, but three frogs hopped away. How many frogs were left?
subtract 9 frogs

There are nine flowers growing by the pond. Each flower has two leaves. How many leaves are there?
multiply 18 leaves

A tree had seven squirrels playing in it. Then, eight more came along. How many squirrels are there in all?
add 15 squirrels

There were 27 birds living in the trees around the pond, but nine flew away. How many birds are left?
subtract 18 birds

One Step Further
Find some flowers around your home. How many petals are on the flowers?

Second Grade Essentials

Second Grade Essentials

ANSWER KEY

248

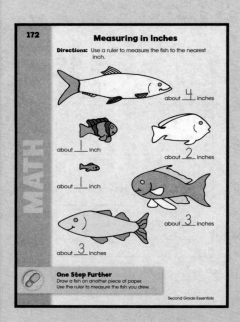

172 — **Measuring in Inches**

Directions: Use a ruler to measure the fish to the nearest inch.

about **4** inches

about **1** inch

about **2** inches

about **1** inch

about **3** inches

about **3** inches

One Step Further
Draw a fish on another piece of paper.
Use the ruler to measure the fish you drew.

Second Grade Essentials

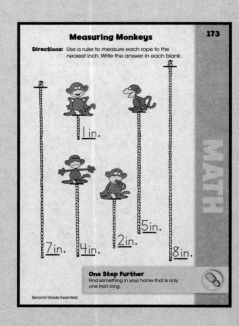

173 — **Measuring Monkeys**

Directions: Use a ruler to measure each rope to the nearest inch. Write the answer in each blank.

1 in.

5 in.

7 in. **4** in. **2** in. **8** in.

One Step Further
Find something in your home that is only one inch long.

Second Grade Essentials

174 — **Measuring in Centimeters**

Directions: Use a centimeter ruler to find the height or the length of the objects below. Write the answer in each blank.

Example:

11 cm

centimeters

9 cm

4 cm

5 cm **2** cm **15** cm

One Step Further
What is the tallest zoo animal you can think of? What is the longest?

Second Grade Essentials

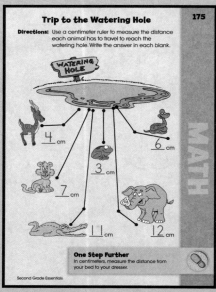

175 — **Trip to the Watering Hole**

Directions: Use a centimeter ruler to measure the distance each animal has to travel to reach the watering hole. Write the answer in each blank.

WATERING HOLE

4 cm

6 cm

3 cm

7 cm

11 cm **12** cm

One Step Further
In centimeters, measure the distance from your bed to your dresser.

Second Grade Essentials

176 — **Whole and Half**

A **fraction** is a number that names part of a whole, such as ½.

Directions: Color half of each thing.

Example: whole apple half an apple

One Step Further
Divide a piece of toast into two equal halves.
Eat one half. How much is left?

Second Grade Essentials

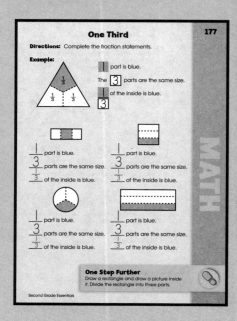

177 — **One Third**

Directions: Complete the fraction statements.

Example:

$\frac{1}{3}$

$\frac{1}{3}$ $\frac{1}{3}$

1 part is blue.
The **3** parts are the same size.
1 of the inside is blue.
3

$\frac{1}{3}$ part is blue.
$\frac{1}{3}$ parts are the same size.
$\frac{1}{3}$ of the inside is blue.

$\frac{1}{3}$ part is blue.
$\frac{1}{3}$ parts are the same size.
$\frac{1}{3}$ of the inside is blue.

$\frac{1}{3}$ part is blue.
$\frac{1}{3}$ parts are the same size.
$\frac{1}{3}$ of the inside is blue.

$\frac{1}{3}$ part is blue.
$\frac{1}{3}$ parts are the same size.
$\frac{1}{3}$ of the inside is blue.

One Step Further
Draw a rectangle and draw a picture inside it. Divide the rectangle into three parts.

Second Grade Essentials

ANSWER KEY

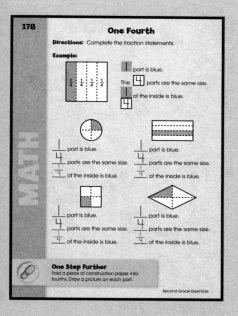

178 — One Fourth

Directions: Complete the fraction statements.

Example:

$\frac{1}{4}$ part is blue.
The $\frac{?}{4}$ parts are the same size.
$\frac{?}{4}$ of the inside is blue.

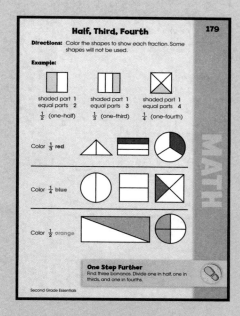

179 — Half, Third, Fourth

Directions: Color the shapes to show each fraction. Some shapes will not be used.

Example:

shaded part 1 / equal parts 2 — $\frac{1}{2}$ (one-half)
shaded part 1 / equal parts 3 — $\frac{1}{3}$ (one-third)
shaded part 1 / equal parts 4 — $\frac{1}{4}$ (one-fourth)

Color $\frac{1}{3}$ red
Color $\frac{1}{4}$ blue
Color $\frac{1}{2}$ orange

One Step Further
Find three bananas. Divide one in half, one in thirds, and one in fourths.

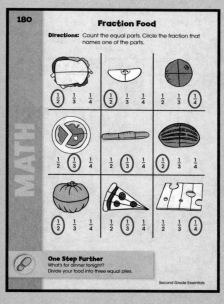

180 — Fraction Food

Directions: Count the equal parts. Circle the fraction that names one of the parts.

One Step Further
What's for dinner tonight? Divide your food into three equal piles.

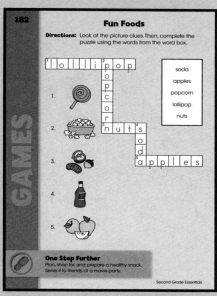

182 — Fun Foods

Directions: Look at the picture clues. Then, complete the puzzle using the words from the word box.

Word box: soda, apples, popcorn, lollipop, nuts

1. lollipop
2. nuts
3. apples

One Step Further
Plan, shop for, and prepare a healthy snack. Serve it to friends at a movie party.

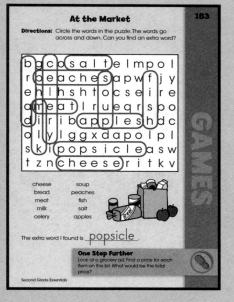

183 — At the Market

Directions: Circle the words in the puzzle. The words go across and down. Can you find an extra word?

cheese, bread, meat, milk, celery, soup, peaches, fish, salt, apples

The extra word I found is _popsicle_

One Step Further
Look at a grocery ad. Find a price for each item on the list. What would be the total price?

184 — Awesome Animals

Directions: Circle the words in the puzzle. The words go across and down.

elephant, giraffe, alligator, dolphin, turtle, horse, whale, snake, zebra, monkey

One Step Further
Use toys to make a zoo. Make a sign for each animal enclosure and a map for guests.

Amphibians and Reptiles
185

Directions: Read the clues and use the words in the word box to complete the puzzle.

Word box: amphibian, reptile, turtle, crocodile, frog

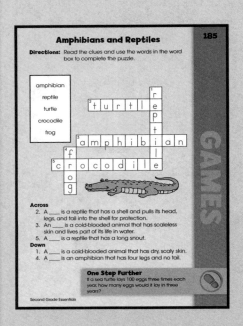

Crossword answers: turtle, amphibian, crocodile, frog, reptile

Across
2. A ___ is a reptile that has a shell and pulls its head, legs, and tail into the shell for protection.
3. An ___ is a cold-blooded animal that has scaleless skin and lives part of its life in water.
5. A ___ is a reptile that has a long snout.

Down
1. A ___ is a cold-blooded animal that has dry, scaly skin.
4. A ___ is an amphibian that has four legs and no tail.

One Step Further
If a sea turtle lays 100 eggs three times each year, how many eggs would it lay in three years?

Second Grade Essentials

186
Time for a Scrub!

Directions: Help the robin find the birdbath.

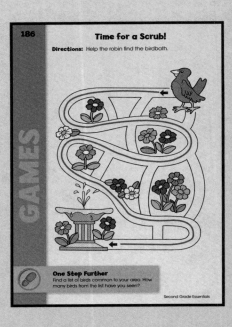

One Step Further
Find a list of birds common to your area. How many birds from the list have you seen?

Second Grade Essentials

For the Birds
187

Directions: Fit the bird words from the cloud into the puzzle.

Answers: jay, owl, eagle, robin, parrots, ostrich, pigeons, buzzard

Cloud: buzzard, robin, jay, parrots, pigeons, eagle, ostrich, owl

One Step Further
Roll a stale bagel in peanut butter and bird-seed. Tie it to a branch outside for the birds.

Second Grade Essentials

188
Here Kitty Kitty!

Directions: See how many times you find the word **kitty** in the puzzle. Color the boxes to show the word. Be sure to look down and across.

k	i	y	k	i	t	t	y	k
i	t	k	i	t	t	y	t	t
k	i	t	t	y	y	i	k	t
i	t	y	t	k	i	t	t	y
y	t	k	y	k	i	t	t	y

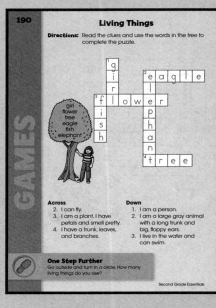

One Step Further
The Spanish word for **cat** is **el gato**. Learn how to say **cat** in another language.

Second Grade Essentials

Little Ones
189

Directions: Look at the picture clues. Then, complete the puzzle using the words from the word box.

Answers: duckling, chick, cub, puppies, colt, kittens

Word box: puppies, cub, duckling, chick, kittens, colt

One Step Further
A baby deer is a fawn. A baby goose is a gosling. Find three more baby animal names.

Second Grade Essentials

190
Living Things

Directions: Read the clues and use the words in the tree to complete the puzzle.

Tree words: girl, flower, tree, eagle, fish, elephant

Answers: girl, eagle, flower, elephant, fish, tree

Across
2. I can fly.
3. I am a plant. I have petals and smell pretty.
4. I have a trunk, leaves, and branches.

Down
1. I am a person.
2. I am a large gray animal with a long trunk and big, floppy ears.
3. I live in the water and can swim.

One Step Further
Go outside and turn in a circle. How many living things do you see?

Second Grade Essentials

ANSWER KEY

Second Grade Essentials

Nonliving Things 191

Directions: Read the clues and use the words in the word box to complete the puzzle.

Word box: chair, ball, telephone, bicycle, swing, sweater

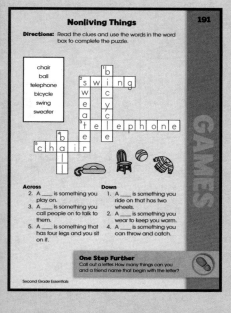

Crossword answers:
- 2 across: **swing**
- 3 across: **telephone**
- 5 across: **chair**
- 1 down: **bicycle**
- 2 down: **sweater**
- 4 down: **ball**

Across
2. A ___ is something you play on.
3. A ___ is something you call people on to talk to them.
5. A ___ is something that has four legs and you sit on it.

Down
1. A ___ is something you ride on that has two wheels.
2. A ___ is something you wear to keep you warm.
4. A ___ is something you can throw and catch.

One Step Further
Call out a letter. How many things can you and a friend name that begin with the letter?

Second Grade Essentials

A Final Question 192

Directions: Match the scrambled letters to find out what the farmer wants to ask.

What's in the big red barn?

1 2 3 4 5 6 7 8 9 10 11 12 13 14 15 16 17 18 19 20 21

One Step Further
How would you spend your day on a farm? Write a schedule for each hour of the day.

Second Grade Essentials

Barnyard Adventure 193

Directions: Help the children get to the barn.

One Step Further
What would be your favorite chore to do on a farm? Why?

Second Grade Essentials

Bath Time 194

Directions: Help the boy get to the bathtub.

One Step Further
Get a bucket of soapy water and a sponge. Use them to wash your bike, toys, or dog!

Second Grade Essentials

In the Bathroom 195

Directions: Circle the words in the puzzle. The words go across, down, and diagonally.

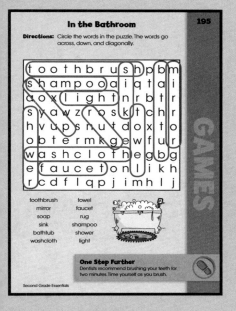

toothbrush, towel, mirror, faucet, soap, rug, sink, shampoo, bathtub, shower, washcloth, light

One Step Further
Dentists recommend brushing your teeth for two minutes. Time yourself as you brush.

Second Grade Essentials

Pet Time 196

Directions: Look in the bone for the things you might need for a new pet. Write the words in the puzzle.

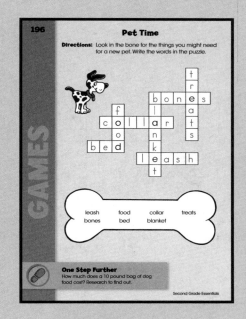

Crossword answers: treats, bones, collar, food, bed, leash, blanket

Bone word box: leash, food, collar, treats, bones, bed, blanket

One Step Further
How much does a 10 pound bag of dog food cost? Research to find out.

Second Grade Essentials

ANSWER KEY

ANSWER KEY

Where's the Bone? — 197

Directions: Help the dog find the bone.

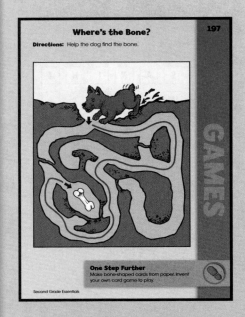

One Step Further
Make bone-shaped cards from paper. Invent your own card game to play.

Second Grade Essentials

Fish — 198

Directions: Read the clues and use the words in the word box to complete the puzzle.

colors
lakes
mouths
ocean
fins
gills

Crossword answers:
1. o c e a n
2. c o l o r s (down)
3. m o u t h s
4. g i l l s
5. l a k e s (down)
6. f i n s

Across
1. Saltwater fish live in the ____.
3. Fish open and close their ____ as they swim to get air from the water.
4. The water comes out of their ____.
6. Fish have tails and ____.

Down
2. Fish are many different sizes, shapes, and ____.
5. Freshwater fish live in ponds, rivers, or ____.

One Step Further
Cut fish shapes from colored paper. Write a math fact on each one.

Second Grade Essentials

Spouting About — 199

Directions: To find the mystery letter, color the spaces with the following letters.

e m c q y r o j a

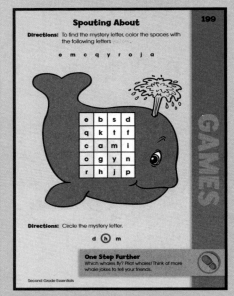

Letter grid:
e	b	s	d
q	k	t	f
c	a	m	l
o	g	y	n
r	h	j	p

Directions: Circle the mystery letter.

d (h) m

One Step Further
Which whales fly? Pilot whales! Think of more whale jokes to tell your friends.

Second Grade Essentials

Fruity Fun — 200

Directions: Read the word for each picture. Write the words in the puzzle.

Crossword answers:
1. o r a n g e (down)
2. p l u m
3. a p p l e
4. p e a c h (down)
5. g r a p e s

Across
2. plum
3. apple
5. grapes

Down
1. orange
2. pear
4. peach

One Step Further
Mix up a smoothie. Use at least two different fruits. Write your recipe.

Second Grade Essentials

Plants We Eat — 201

Directions: Read the clues and use the words in the word box to complete the puzzle.

carrot
rhubarb
lettuce
corn
peach

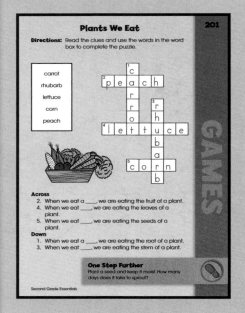

Crossword answers:
1. c a r r o t (down)
2. p e a c h
3. r h u b a r b (down)
4. l e t t u c e
5. c o r n

Across
2. When we eat a ____, we are eating the fruit of a plant.
4. When we eat ____, we are eating the leaves of a plant.
5. When we eat ____, we are eating the seeds of a plant.

Down
1. When we eat a ____, we are eating the root of a plant.
3. When we eat ____, we are eating the stem of a plant.

One Step Further
Plant a seed and keep it moist. How many days does it take to sprout?

Second Grade Essentials

Land and Water — 202

Directions: Read the clues and use the words in the word box to complete the puzzle.

Crossword answers:
1. p l a i n (down)
2. l a k e
4. m o u n t a i n
3. r i v e r / v a l l e y
5. o c e a n (down)

mountain
valley
plain
ocean
lake
river

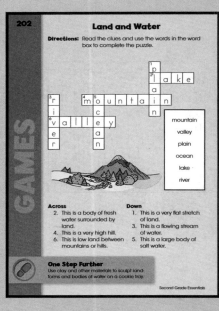

Across
2. This is a body of fresh water surrounded by land.
4. This is a very high hill.
6. This is low land between mountains or hills.

Down
1. This is a very flat stretch of land.
3. This is a flowing stream of water.
5. This is a large body of salt water.

One Step Further
Use clay and other materials to sculpt landforms and bodies of water on a cookie tray.

Second Grade Essentials

Out in Space — 203

Directions: On the lines, write the name of the object shown in the picture.

1. P l u t o
2. m o o n
3. S a t u r n
4. r o c k e t
5. s t a r
6. E a r t h
7. c o m e t
8. V e n u s

| star | Earth | rocket | Pluto |
| moon | comet | Saturn | Venus |

One Step Further
Choose one planet in our solar system. Learn three facts about it.

Second Grade Essentials

Forest Life — 204

Directions: Read the clues and use the words in the word box to complete the puzzle.

sunlight
insects
squirrels
forest
trees
deer

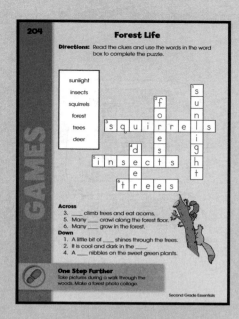

Crossword answers:
- s q u i r r e l s
- s u n l i g h t
- f o r e s t
- d e e r
- i n s e c t s
- t r e e s

Across
3. ____ climb trees and eat acorns.
5. Many ____ crawl along the forest floor.
6. Many ____ grow in the forest.

Down
1. A little bit of ____ shines through the trees.
2. It is cool and dark in the ____.
4. A ____ nibbles on the sweet green plants.

One Step Further
Take pictures during a walk through the woods. Make a forest photo collage.

Second Grade Essentials

Busy Beaver — 205

Directions: Help the beaver find the water.

One Step Further
What does "busy as a beaver" mean? What other animal sayings can you think of?

Second Grade Essentials

Squaring Up — 206

Directions: Use a word from the box to complete each sentence. Then, write each word in the puzzle.

| kite |
| caps |
| snake |
| clock |

Crossword:
- c l o c k
- c a p
- k i t
- s n a k e

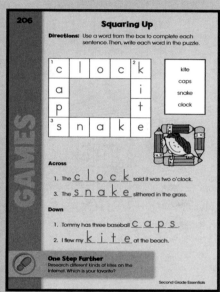

Across
1. The c l o c k said it was two o'clock.
3. The s n a k e slithered in the grass.

Down
1. Tommy has three baseball c a p s.
2. I flew my k i t e at the beach.

One Step Further
Research different kinds of kites on the Internet. Which is your favorite?

Second Grade Essentials

In the Desk — 207

Directions: Circle the words in the puzzle. The words go across and down.

j o p e n c i l m n g t c l
n f a n b f c x r x e a r p
l a p v e r a s e r m p a a
k p e n o v c x w k o e y i
m k r s t a p l e r v r o n
f r e l m n i j n b t n n t
m n o t e b o o k m h n s s
v r d c j o l p l o m n b f

pencil   pen
paper   eraser
stapler   paints
crayons   tape
notebook

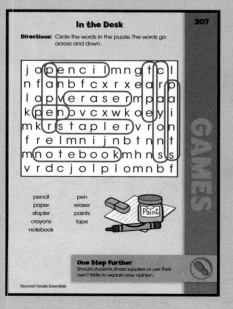

One Step Further
Should students share supplies or use their own? Write to explain your opinion.

Second Grade Essentials

School Days — 208

Directions: Circle the words in the puzzle. The words go across, down, and diagonally.

p t k l r t e a c h e r t
u a e r a s e r r u t s s
g f p m q n o p a d e s c
h j p e n c i l y r s v i
g e i y r h a w o p t h s
v l x z z a d x n q g i s
w d u c y l e b s f k j o
b a d e s k p a i n t r
c o m p u t e r l m o n s

paper   eraser   glue
pencil   chalk   scissors
test   crayons   teacher
desk   paint   computer

One Step Further
Design an activity for your class. What supplies would you need? Share with your teacher.

Second Grade Essentials

ANSWER KEY

GAMES

254

ANSWER KEY

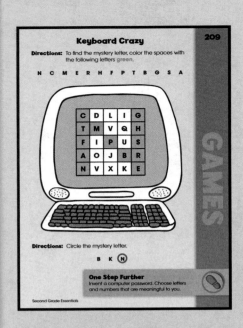

Keyboard Crazy 209

Directions: To find the mystery letter, color the spaces with the following letters green.

N C M E R H F P T B G S A

C	D	L	I	G
T	M	V	Q	H
F	I	P	U	S
A	O	J	B	R
N	V	X	K	E

Directions: Circle the mystery letter.

B K (N)

One Step Further
Invent a computer password. Choose letters and numbers that are meaningful to you.

Second Grade Essentials

GAMES

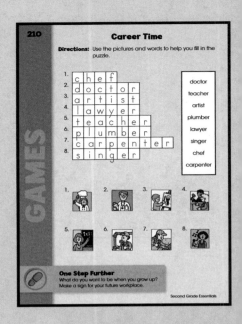

Career Time 210

Directions: Use the pictures and words to help you fill in the puzzle.

1. chef
2. doctor
3. artist
4. lawyer
5. teacher
6. plumber
7. carpenter
8. singer

doctor
teacher
artist
plumber
lawyer
singer
chef
carpenter

1. 2. 3. 4.
5. 6. 7. 8.

One Step Further
What do you want to be when you grow up? Make a sign for your future workplace.

Second Grade Essentials

GAMES

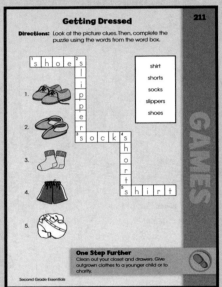

Getting Dressed 211

Directions: Look at the picture clues. Then, complete the puzzle using the words from the word box.

s h o e s
l i p p e r
s o c k s h o r t s h i r t

shirt
shorts
socks
slippers
shoes

1.
2.
3.
4.
5.

One Step Further
Clean out your closet and drawers. Give outgrown clothes to a younger child or to charity.

Second Grade Essentials

GAMES

Fly Away Home 212

Directions: Help the butterfly find the butterfly house.

One Step Further
Draw the life stages of a butterfly: egg, caterpillar, chrysalis, adult.

Second Grade Essentials

GAMES

Second Grade Essentials

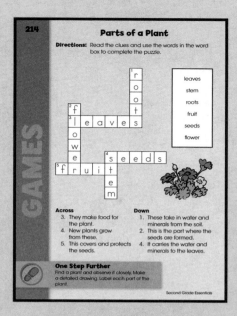

At the Pond
213

Directions: Read the clues and use the words in the word box to complete the puzzle.

Word box: cattails, lily pad, turtle, fish, willow, pond

Crossword answers:
- 1 Down: turtle
- 2 Down: willow
- 3 Down: cattails
- 4 Across: lily pad
- 5 Across: pond
- 6 Across: fish

Across
4. A bullfrog sits on a ____ and croaks a loud song.
5. A family of ducks waddle into the ____ for a swim.
6. A raccoon tries to catch a ____ as it swims by.

Down
1. A ____ sits on a rock in the morning sun.
2. The weeping ____ gives shade to the animals.
3. Birds fly over the many ____ sticking out of the water.

One Step Further
Take a magnifying glass to a pond or stream near you. What do you see?

Second Grade Essentials

Parts of a Plant
214

Directions: Read the clues and use the words in the word box to complete the puzzle.

Word box: leaves, stem, roots, fruit, seeds, flower

Crossword answers:
- 1 Down: root
- 2 Down: flower
- 3 Across: leaves
- 4 Down: stem
- 5 Across: fruit / seeds

Across
3. They make food for the plant.
4. New plants grow from these.
5. This covers and protects the seeds.

Down
1. These take in water and minerals from the soil.
2. This is the part where the seeds are formed.
4. It carries the water and minerals to the leaves.

One Step Further
Find a plant and observe it closely. Make a detailed drawing. Label each part of the plant.

Second Grade Essentials

In My Garden
215

Directions: Circle the words in the puzzle. The words go across and down.

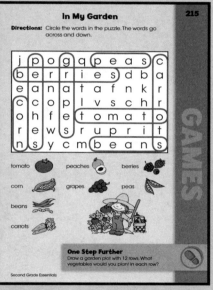

Word search grid:
```
j p o g q p e a s c
b e r r i e s d b a
e a n a t a f n k r
c c o p l v s c h r
o h f e t o m a t o
r e w s r u p r i t
n s y c m b e a n s
```

tomato, peaches, berries, corn, grapes, peas, beans, carrots

One Step Further
Draw a garden plot with 12 rows. What vegetables would you plant in each row?

Second Grade Essentials

What's the Mystery?
216

Directions: Use the pictures to help you fill in the puzzle. Then, use the words you wrote in the sentences below.

Word box: leak, lock, mail, meal

Crossword answers:
- 1 Across: meal
- 1 Down: mail
- 2 Down: leak
- 3 Across: lock

Across
1. He ate the m e a l.
3. The l o c k is on the door.

Down
1. Please open the m a i l.
2. Does that pipe l e a k?

One Step Further
Give a friend three clues to a number. Can your friend guess the number?

Second Grade Essentials

256

ANSWER KEY

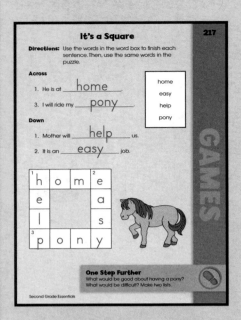

It's a Square 217

Directions: Use the words in the word box to finish each sentence. Then, use the same words in the puzzle.

Across

1. He is at ___home___

3. I will ride my ___pony___

Down

1. Mother will ___help___ us.

2. It is an ___easy___ job.

Word box: home, easy, help, pony

Puzzle:
1. h o m e
   e   a
   l   s
3. p o n y

One Step Further
What would be good about having a pony? What would be difficult? Make two lists.

Second Grade Essentials

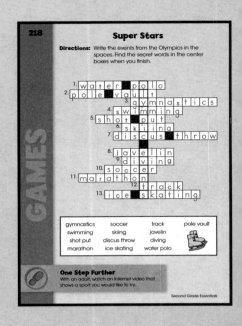

218 **Super Stars**

Directions: Write the events from the Olympics in the spaces. Find the secret words in the center boxes when you finish.

1. water polo
2. pole vault
3. gymnastics
4. swimming
5. shot put
6. skiing
7. discus throw
8. javelin
9. diving
10. soccer
11. marathon
12. track
13. ice skating

Word box:
gymnastics, soccer, track, pole vault, swimming, skiing, javelin, shot put, discus throw, diving, marathon, ice skating, water polo

One Step Further
With an adult, watch an Internet video that shows a sport you would like to try.

Second Grade Essentials

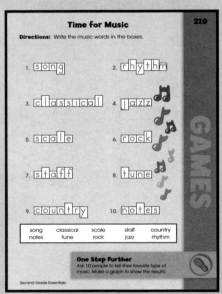

Time for Music 219

Directions: Write the music words in the boxes.

1. song
2. rhythm
3. classical
4. jazz
5. scale
6. rock
7. staff
8. tune
9. country
10. notes

Word box: song, classical, scale, staff, country, notes, tune, rock, jazz, rhythm

One Step Further
Ask 10 people to tell their favorite type of music. Make a graph to show the results.

Second Grade Essentials

Second Grade Essentials